Parag Saigaonkar is a Principal with Deloitte Consulting working in the India market. From 2005 to July 2013, Parag was the Regional Managing Director for the firm's global off-shore consulting services out of India during which time he helped grow the practice from a few hundred to several thousand professionals across several offices in India.

Parag began his career with the firm in 1990. In 1995, he moved to Hong Kong and later, also had a stint in Beijing. Parag moved from Beijing to Mumbai in April 2005 where he presently lives with his wife Vandana and his two sons Pranav and Arjun.

When he is not pursuing clients, Parag likes to spend time with his family, mostly negotiating deals between his two boys. Most feuds at home have been taken care of by his specially prepared pasta or a quick road trip to Pune. His mental notes about people and situations around him led him to blogging at first, and later to *The Perfect Storm*.

The
Perfect
Storm

Are you the New India Manager?

By

Parag Saigaonkar

𝓌

westland ltd

61, II Floor, Silverline Building, Alapakkam Main Road, Maduravoyal, Chennai 600095
93, I Floor, Sham Lal Road, Daryaganj, New Delhi 110002

First published by westland ltd 2014

Copyright © Parag Saigaonkar 2014

10 9 8 7 6 5 4 3 2 1

ISBN : 978-93-84030-71-1

Typeset by PrePSol Enterprises Pvt. Ltd.

Printed at Thomson Press

To my parents for their courage to chart unknown waters; Vandana for being my anchor and steer; Pranav and Arjun – my north stars

Table of Contents

Foreword   **xi**

Preface   **xiii**

PART 1 – Understanding the nature of the storm

    1.1   *Eastward Ho – Where the puck is going*   **3**

    1.2   *Forces At Play – What this storm is all about*   **17**

    1.3   *The Corporate Workplace – Move away bare beige walls*   **31**

    Blogs   **36**

- Gen Y or Gen Whine?
- The Freshmen and the Family
- The Slave Driver, the Intellectual, the Army General, the Diplomat and me – Be a mentor
- Dog Fight is Here. Are you Ready?
- The Tipping Point
- Where have all the leaders gone?

PART 2 – 'Working Through' the eye of the storm

    2.1   *The Storm and the Long Haul*   **57**

Blogs   **65**

- ❑   Life is Short, careers run long
- ❑   Sine Curve Theory
- ❑   What's in a Title
- ❑   Kandinsky and Immersion
- ❑   Keep Paddling, Calm Waters Ahead

**2.2   Sailing Skills – Choose well, stay put,
        navigate small trips**   **78**

Blogs   **90**

- ❑   Eggs and Oranges?
- ❑   Every Day Can't be a Monday
- ❑   Spilt Milk and a Shrug
- ❑   Lessons from an Envelope
- ❑   Don't Chase Work-Life balance – Long Haul, Stay
      Connected
- ❑   When Yes means Maybe
- ❑   That 25 Percent

**2.3   The Mettle That Turns The Course – Looking
        inwards in rapidly changing waters**   **107**

Blogs   **115**

- ❑   Find the Gap and Take the Lunge
- ❑   The Bamboo that Bends
- ❑   Rugby and the Good Leg
- ❑   Will we really go through the clouds?
- ❑   Chuck the Agenda and Say Hello
- ❑   To Sign the Chit or Not To

- ❏ Do you have an expensive signature?
- ❏ My Recipe for Success

Part 3 – The New India Manager

3.1	**Breaking Through to 'Managerhood'**	**139**
3.2	**Women at the Helm**	**150**

Blogs   155

- ❏ Taking off the Blinders
- ❏ The Global Nomad
- ❏ Be the breakthrough, not barrier
- ❏ So, who is this New Manager?
- ❏ The Curious Case of Manav Anand
- ❏ Breaking Through the clouds
- ❏ Blue Collar Leader

PART 4 – Leadership and Next

4.1	**Leaders Ahoy!**	**175**

Blogs   187

- ❏ Tell Me Your Story, All Calls on Hold – Empathy
- ❏ The Green Jacket – The intangibles
- ❏ The Sirius Effect – Charisma
- ❏ Spidey's Right
- ❏ The Shackleton Odyssey – In the face of challenge
- ❏ Walking the Fields of Gettysburg – brevity and powerful conversations
- ❏ Home Truths about People Management

4.2 *Final Reflections* – What next? Who next? 205

Gaudi's Canvas – The job is never done 211

Afterword 213

Acknowledgements 215

Foreword

People often call India a "talent goldmine." That's a pretty big claim, but as a Talent executive for a large U.S. organization that's been operating in India for over a dozen years, I have been amazed at just how true it is. In fact, it's hard to overstate the quality of talented people in India. Our Indian employees are invariably innovative, flexible, smart, and incredibly hard-working. A rich vein of gold, indeed.

So, yes, India is a "goldmine" of talent. But mining gold takes time, patience, and effort. Likewise, helping the talented people of India to shine requires a lot of understanding on both sides, as well as trust and hard work. Because our goal isn't just to find "talent gold" – we want to help our colleagues in India develop and grow. Just as we do for our U.S.-based employees, we want to create conditions in which they can thrive as leaders.

Indian history is, of course, rich and deep, and Western managers have a steep learning curve to understand the environment, social pressures, and desires of the young people who comprise the majority of this remarkable talent pool. I should add that this isn't strictly an East/West issue. Even managers who've spent their whole lives in India have trouble figuring out the young people of India's Gen Y, who grew up under very different circumstances than their parents.

And Indian professionals wanting to advance into leadership in Western companies need to seek out mentors who understand today's business culture in India. Those mentors may be hard to find because the culture has shifted significantly in just the space of a generation or two. A 21-year-old entering the world of work in India today has very different needs and wants from his or her Western peers, but they're also different than those of an Indian beginning a career 30 or 40 years ago. The pioneering young people creating modern India's business culture need pioneering mentors – people with wide perspectives, who can assimilate a diverse range of ideas and styles of doing business and translate that knowledge in a way that can help India's young leaders thrive.

Parag Saigaonkar has a unique perspective on these issues. As an Indian expat turned "re-pat", he's seen the business world from both the Eastern and the Western perspectives. And he has some valuable advice for all of us doing business in India – whether we're "miners" or "gold," organizations or talent.

Jennifer Steinmann
Chief Talent Officer, Deloitte LLP

Preface

In September 1970, I left India on a Toronto bound Swiss Air flight for my 'new home in Canada' with my mother and older brother. I was four years old. It was only years later that I came to know how much of a risk my father had taken by emigrating to a foreign land in search of a good life for his children.

When we left, my father still had no secure job at hand even though he had left a few months earlier in order to 'arrange' for a job and abode for his family. It was a huge, huge risk and one that had no precedent in the family. We were, for a long time, the only family unit, within an extremely close knit traditional Maharashtrian extended family, to have migrated overseas.

So, when I did return back to India thirty five years later to work (via a nine year stint in Hong Kong and Beijing), the mini adjustments that my family and I had to make around traffic, weather, spices, and school admissions, though challenging, were trivial in comparison to the trepidations my father probably bore in his initial years in a place so far away from home.

For me, it was just coming back 'home' again with a little bit of an expat mindset woven in. Simple.

Year 2005 - India was on the move: economy and confidence surging, largest youth population, impressive English speaking man power, deep pool of professionals and technocrats set to become the service provider of the world. With an average age of 25-26, ten years younger than China and twenty behind the western world, this was the harbinger of what could be a very Indian century.

India was the source and destination for talent. And my job at hand was to lead a team of around 500 of these young professionals. These *Gen Yers* (cohort of those born 1980-onwards) filled out the work place with a few *Gen Xs* (those born between the early 1960s and 1980) sitting around the office in their corner cabins. By the way, my office was pitched up as a symbolic 'fish bowl' in the middle of the floor. The *Gen Ys* were a generation very different from the baby boomers (born between 1946 and the early 1960s) and perhaps even the *Gen Xs* when it came to work ethics, skill sets, expectations, goals, dilemmas etc.

And it is precisely this 'otherness' that keeps me curious.

Since 2005, I have watched India and Indians up close, interacted with them, learnt a great deal about them and learnt a great deal from them. Also, I have in my role attempted to share my own observations with them too.

One of the best parts of my job, as an organizational leader, has been visiting campuses all over India and meeting in person these *Gen Yers*, the so called 'demographic dividend', India's ticket to economic prosperity. At campuses, I typically start my introductory talks by telling the students that they have

"...won the parental lottery!" And that they should go home and firstly thank their parents for being born at the right time and at the right place. The best time in modern Indian history!

I tell them how they are the 'poster children', having gone through life with minimum challenges, as their parents have protected them and provided them the best they could. I mostly meet students who have throughout their lives scored at the top of their classes in school, won admission to the best of colleges, graduated from leading universities. The next filter for them would be getting an offer from a company like ours and that guaranteed them a spot at the very tip of the 'dividend iceberg'.

It is a time of transition for India, and times of major transitions precipitate into what I like to refer to as a *Perfect Storm*.

Like in a natural phenomenon, certain forces/trends are converging and hitting the job market and the work places — offering both opportunities and challenges. In India the 'forces' are perhaps – ongoing economic turbulence, the paradox of the 'unemployable graduates', a very young, knowledge-intensive, highly mobile and diverse work-force, the need for up-skilling (soft-skills), need for mentors, nascent industry knowledge and stubbornly evolving social pressures, etc.

The challenge is that while this group is well equipped to take on the world, they have entered the *Perfect Storm*. They would need to navigate the next 40 years or so of professional life, in this turbulent sea, which will not be very easy. Out of colleges, raised on social media, weaned on success, juggling with campus-corporate integration, bombarded with choices or the lack of them, in need of mentors and inspiration, this group would need to navigate the rough seas, and harbour their planned destination, leadership, safe. As they make their way through the manager ranks and hopefully into leadership, there will be several obstacles and unfortunately, they will at some point work with managers and other leaders who might be misaligned in thinking with theirs.

On the upside, this may be the best period in the history of the world to be imagining and preparing for a career. Also, this group will also have a global agenda as India takes its rightful position in the global hierarchy. On the downside, if this pinnacle of the pyramid does not somehow make it, the consequences will be disastrous for them individually and for India as whole.

I landed in India in the middle of this Perfect Storm. My previous brush with India was limited to those long summer vacations in the late 70s and early 80s (every two-three years) I spent with my cousins – riding borrowed bicycles in the by-lanes of Pune, playing gully cricket, attending solemn marriage ceremonies, hurricane tours of tens of destinations that my father insisted we do in order to "...see as much of India as possible". Of course, my parents did a great job throughout of keeping us 'closely linked' with India – my brother and I spoke Marathi (proudly with a 'mild' Canadian accent), relished our poha and puran polis, celebrated Ganapati and tried to carry this ecosystem back to Canada as much as possible. Throughout it all, these intentions allowed us to keep more than just a cultural but a very personal connection to India, allowing me to think about potentially coming back to this land.

After spending nine years in the Asia Pacific region (and consequently developing a bit of China fatigue) it was natural that I slowly started to gravitate towards India. I had not experienced India with a 'business' lens earlier. However, one thing struck me, that amidst those *"Nothing works here!"* moments, were the loads of potential opportunities. One of them was clearly the young, bright and vibrant people around me. It became clear to me that I would need to connect with and soak up every conversation and situation of this group in order to be able to lead them.

And over the last eight years, I have had several conversations with colleagues, new recruits, seniors and longer tenured employees who would approach me with very unique stories and situations about their professional careers and aspirations. I started making mental notes and then real ones. It was now time to reach out to this 'tip of the demographic dividend' crowd. One critical dimension that I wanted to tackle was to make the journey for these new recruits from where they were today to, let's say, a leadership role … achievable. It shouldn't feel an ocean away else I felt that they would simply drift. I had seen life on the other side and was privileged to have an opportunity to better understand their perspectives.

And then I discovered the power of blogging — a *eureka* moment for a person who has shied away from the sensations of social media. I started recording my interactions and conversations in a series of monthly blogs that would be both a bit personal but essentially synthesize some take-aways or mentoring suggestions … many times leveraging personal incidents … into easily understandable lessons. While I did enjoy writing earlier, it was much more in the context of consulting reports versus actual prose and clearly I never imagined that the journey I had embarked on would eventually lead me to actually compile a book.

The ambitious idea of authoring a book came about after being declared a 'blog veteran' by friends and well-wishers. I thought that it would be good to build a narrative around the many blogs I had written on various corporate issues that I was involved in and happened to observe.

This has led to this effort. The book has four sections:

1. Part 1 and 2 set the context of the *Perfect Storm*. The workplace in India today is a melting pot of challenges and opportunities. All the forces are at play both at work and at home, a few beyond control. Can you get your bearings straight and understand the overall context?

2. Part 3 focusses on how to navigate to become 'the New India Manager'. Those who will now propel India to the next level of

economic prosperity. Those cutting their teeth in challenging times and have been able to navigate the course. This is a challenging but rewarding journey but it is setting you up for the final push for leadership. Can you survive the course?

3. Part 4 focusses on leadership. India will need several of these types in the future. So will the world. And given the demographic dividend, there is more responsibility on Indians to make their mark during their journey and at the end of the road. There are a few examples currently, but India has the potential to create many more. Are you one of them?

It has been a long journey for me ... returning 'home'. While Canadian ice hockey still rules my heart, the French I learned in school comes handy on vacations in Europe and my laboriously learnt Mandarin still holds good (though only enough to impress my friends in Mumbai!).... It's India where I clearly see the promise of tomorrow, though I am still working on my Hindi. And this tomorrow is in the hands of this 'tip of the iceberg'. I am a huge optimist and the morning news about corruption, inflation and blackouts can't deter my spirit. These I believe are only ripples frankly given the news that one hears in countries across many parts of Asia. India indeed is a miracle in my mind. The largest democracy in the world, in a chaotic geopolitical environment, churning out thousands of English-speaking skilled graduates. And this generation needs to lead it to its deserved destination.

Now we need to do all we can to make sure that this 'generation of hope' succeeds in navigating not just the current version of India but a future vision that will be significantly different from what we see today.

It is said that a *Perfect Storm* moment is perhaps a once in a life time moment. The storm is perfect because you are ready for it.

Let's set sail....

PART 1

Understanding the nature of the storm

To reach a port we must set sail, sail, not drift.

1.1   Eastward Ho – Where the puck is going

The fog's just lifting. Throw off your bow line; throw off your stern.

When I landed at Mumbai airport on a sultry April evening in 2005, I knew that this time it was for a very long haul.

Many years ago when my family and I were visiting our extended family in India (my father insisted it be a regular ritual), I recall an old uncle ask my brother and me – *"So do you like coming here from Canada?"* As if we had an option! As children thankfully we never rationalized, but the fact that from the moment we landed we were never *"dragged around"* by our parents, but got swooped away by cousins and relatives, reuniting with our parents only a few days before heading back to Canada, shows that we did *"fit in"*. So, India was about hanging around with a big group of cousins, aunts and uncles and occasionally visiting their friends. What I remember the most was the pace. Or frankly, the lack of it. The summers in India in the 70s seemed long and languorous (except for those marathon 'get to know India' tours where we covered the north and the south of India at warp speed). Our visits were always in the monsoons, so the mangoes were just done and it was more about climbing trees to pluck guavas.

At Pune, our relatives stayed at *wadas* (traditional Maharastrian tenements) and modest apartments. So, our holidays were about playing cards late into the night, hearing the chatter emerging from the neighbours and sleeping in hallways and terraces. The quarters were cramped and you were always looking for an excuse to get out and explore the city. One summer, my uncle brought home one of the first televisions (EC TV) in the *wada*. In no time, the narrow hallway of the *wada* turned into a movie hall of sorts, neighbours and friends of neighbours pouring in, slippers neatly arranged outside, tea and snacks being distributed on the house, children accommodating each other on the floor, the crowd mesmerized by Marathi skits, *Chaya Geet*, Sunday Hindi movies.....the entire daily broadcast those days was just for a few hours.

Given that my cousins were attending school during those months, my brother and I had to keep busy – so we explored the city, occasionally taking the local trains in Mumbai or riding on borrowed cycles in Pune. Rickshaws and taxis were *expensive* and frankly, looking back, less fun. Evenings, we headed straight to the local pitch for cricket and with my baseball swing I would either hit the ball for a six (homerun in baseball parlance) or get out swinging. I was still figuring out the game.

Another uncle who lived in Dadar used to take us to his office in Worli once in a while and in one of the visits during the 80s he proudly showed us a PC in an air conditioned room the size of a telephone booth. It had the same sacrosanct status as of a Ganapati idol at home! On a follow-up visit, he showed a new office wing that was going up with security badges, air conditioned work spaces and PCs on every desk. So change was happening, albeit slowly ...

Coming to India in those days meant a break from the cold and orderly routine of Canada and diving into warmth and sweet chaos. There was little discussion or even a thought about potentially working in India. Interestingly, I did not even ask nor understand what my uncles actually did on a daily basis at work. What was their routine? What was their motivation? I never came to know how much money they earned. Nor did it matter.

There was a long lull in my visits to India after I started university. The course was five years long with work-terms substituted in for summer breaks. I was more focussed on getting a job rather than spending a vacation in India. I did though know a friend who spent one of those work terms in India at an Indian conglomerate. Her stories in the late 80s though made me cringe at the thought of working there. Bosses were hierarchical, there was no motivation for working extra, no one had heard of mentorship (at best you could be the boss's pet). She told me *"The whole environment is isolating, not based on merit but on some warped up logic of 'in India we are like this only'."*

The declining frequency of calls overseas illustrated how my cousins and I seemed to be drifting apart both physically and mentally. At one point, I was not even sure what they were even doing or where they were working. India was a forgotten hinterland for some time now.

Life at university did though allow me to connect with other friends of Indian origin who had grown up in Canada similar to me. Many of our stories had common themes – Parents migrating to the West even before we learnt to recognize what was around us, then hours of pining for what they had left behind, the attempts to keep 'our great culture' alive in our living rooms, quizzes during dinner on – *"Do you remember Uncle Patil?"*. We kids all pretty much bobbed between many ports. There were a couple though who stood out and openly talked about longer term plans of 'doing something big for India' but for most, India meant *samosas*, wearing *kurtas* or *saris* during a India Students Meet, and sometimes watching Bollywood. Back then, the idea of actually working in India was as distant as working on the moon.

My first job as a consultant in Ottawa made a big impression. My colleagues were exceptional professionals who taught me the difference between getting a job and joining a profession. The latter had a much more longer-term lens while the former simply meant a pay cheque. Becoming a *professional* was a longer term journey. There was responsibility in developing other people and in serving *clients* versus simply catering to customers. We were a *firm* not a company. There were professionals striving to become *partners* (and owners) not simply employees who were waiting for the next opportunity to jump ship. The partners took personal interest in each new consultant. You did not have to look for mentors as they were all around you.

A couple of years into the profession, I realized that an MBA would be required for me to excel in this profession. While I had taken some business courses in undergrad school, I was getting frankly a bit lost in some areas like finance and economics. With my computer science and math background, picking up and reading a business journal was a challenge. This had to change.

The two years at MBA school opened my eyes to an emerging global economy and a plethora of new business-related subjects like being an operating manager, managing a professional services firm and the most sought after – corporate strategy. We had colleagues from around the world and the business school had leadership development programmes in Russia and China. They were clearly trying to make the programme a global experience. Working in Ottawa for federal government clients in hindsight felt like living in a cocoon.

At that time, one of my best friends was from Hong Kong and opened my eyes to Asia and the then termed Asian tiger economies. The city state was one of them. Skyscrapers, financial capital, trading hub and tycoons. He talked about a thriving economy and an incredibly fast pace of life. The British rule made it very easy for foreigners to live and work. Talking and thinking about Hong Kong made India disappear from my grand plans about life and such, as if forever. I even took time out to make a trip out to the Far East on a vacation before starting my MBA just to get a feel for the city and region. It was an amazing experience. Indians in the 70s and 80s were primarily looking west if they had a chance to leave India. Very few ventured east.

Returning back to consulting in Ottawa after the MBA, I realized that I needed to change course. When I had heard that the firm had established a joint-venture in Hong Kong, I was determined to figure out a way to apply. An interview was booked with the managing partner of the joint venture in Toronto and in an hour, I had my job. It was only several months later that I found out that I was the only person across Canada to apply!

I visited India again many times during the late 90s on business, from Hong Kong. Then, the skies were opening up, literally. My first brush with liberalized India was the airline service. Flying had become a completely transformed experience now. Clean planes, friendly staff and timely take-offs and landings. Frankly the service was on par with the other leading Asian carriers and a lot better than back in the West. What impressed me the most was how the new airlines were customizing their service levels for the local population. Every flight served a hot meal (a must for all Indians) with steaming *Idli Sambar*, miniature bottles of *nimbu pani* and perhaps a *gulab jamun* neatly arranged in a small tray. I was once upgraded to business class and here you were treated like a maharaja ... an ocean change from when flying domestically in North America was almost the luck of the draw ... in terms of the flight times and even getting a ticket for a flight – despite the expensive prices.

The paradox was that the modernized domestic airline industry had to work in conjunction with the archaic airport infrastructure. An interesting microcosm of the change happening in India. Some industries were literally taking off (telecom being another) while others (power and utilities) were stuck in a time warp.

During one of those business visits from Hong Kong, when I walked across the street to meet a client, I decided to overlook the rundown infrastructure, the *paan* stains on the dowdy looking elevator lobby, the immitigable Mumbai stench (in Mumbai you can be blindfolded and tell which part of the city you are in by the stink or the fragrance) till I reached the non-working elevators (and this was downtown Mumbai – the main business district!) Anyone visiting India was always hit by the dilapidated state of its infrastructure.

After walking up a few flights of stairs, going through in my mind a few facts I needed to discuss with the team I was supposed to meet, I was surprised to find a couple of senior folks, with whom I presumed we would be having a sombre closed-door meeting, as they were simply having a cup of tea and chatting. I naively narrated my tale about my trudge up the stairs - they gave a shrug and said – *"No electricity, what can you do?"* So, we spent the next few hours simply chatting about politics, Mumbai infrastructure, creative ways of overcoming traffic snarls and power outages! Clearly a very different pace of life from what I had become accustomed to in Hong Kong.

After the power returned, I asked about making a call back to Hong Kong and they pointed me to a fax machine in the corridor. It was the only international dialling line in the office. The elevator and the outdated communications mode did throw me out a bit, but eventually what stayed on for a very long time was the energetic conversation, the audacious dreams of the group I met ..... India was marching on clearly, *sans* a smooth elevator ride.

Honestly, my move to India from China was much prompted by my 'China fatigue'. For close to a decade, nine years in Hong Kong and then one in Beijing, while my family and I thoroughly enjoyed our time, we very much felt like foreigners. The 'expat' like life in Hong Kong was terrific but you realize that you are truly in a foreign land when you step inside an elevator and mentally block out the conversations, because you simply don't understand the language or the context. The morning and weekend Mandarin classes were becoming a grind, let alone fretting over those Chinese instructions on baby food and Chinese charactered DVD remote controls....

Work wise, I was not doing badly – a consultant in telecommunications serving the Asia-Pacific region. The telecom market was de-regulating turning once monopoly-dominated countries into fully competitive environments; Asia was being viewed as Goliath in a cradle. We had a relatively small group of 40-50 consultants in Hong Kong who were extremely busy – and we were also having a lot of fun organizing junk boat trips on the weekends and during dragon boat season, training for the big event at Stanley beach! Friday evenings were all about hanging out having a drink in Lan Kwai Fung. Throughout the time in Hong Kong and China, I kept on thinking about whether the timing was right to make the plunge and move to the sub-continent.

During one more business trip to India, I continued to observe the frustrating business environment and loads of potential opportunities. On one of my trips to Delhi, I was amazed at the nimble network in a place which to an outsider would look frenzied. During this short trip of three days to Delhi, I was able to meet with the CEO of a major telecom company, two-three young telecom consulting start-ups and I was even able to get a meeting with a senior advisor to the communications minister at Rashtrapati Bhavan – all in a span of three days! They told me all that mattered were 'connections'. The 'capital' power was becoming clearer to me. There was a young chap who showed me around for those three days. He seemed to know everyone, though somehow no one really seemed to value his connections. But, I was certainly impressed.

I had started to better understand the subtle differences between the cities in India. In the same trip, I flew down to Bangalore to take some time off and what I saw there was a bustling city, as if getting ready for its digital future...getting ready to be included as a verb in the Western lexicon ... 'Bangalored'! New housing complexes, modern amenities, bungalows in gated communities were a far cry from the *wadas* of Pune. 'My India' – the one I had lived in all those years ago seemed like it was in a time warp.

A year later, another trip brought me to Chennai, a city which I barely remembered – some kind of a holy transit point which we only passed through, some twenty odd years ago, during one of those 'must see India' whirlwind tours. Chennai was clearly not moving at the pace of Bangalore, but there were pockets like the gated communities or some of the bank captive centres supporting global banks. From Chennai, I had to head back to Bangalore for some follow-up meetings with this client, a television manufacturer, which was looking to increase its market share in India's booming consumer electronics market. Visiting some of the shops and speaking with the distributors, it was clear that India had come a long way from the days of my uncle's EC TV.

Foreign competition was driving Indian companies to innovate and new entrants were driving prices down making such previously imagined 'luxury' items into regular household goods. New business models were also being designed to support the different regions, and the consumers (the new-born, half awake, half rising middle class) were lapping it all up.

It was during this trip that I felt that 'one day' it would be a great move to work in India and get better 'connected' with the country of my birth, but I was still not going to sacrifice too much in my career 'just to get to India'. The timing had to be right and the opportunities at that time in the late 90s, things were still maturing.

When my friends and colleagues at Hong Kong first heard about my aspirations to 'go back' to India, they thought it was perhaps a momentary lapse of good judgment. China was where the action was – a point about which I clearly could not disagree. As many of them were keen on moving to North America, they felt it strange that if I ever left Hong Kong why I would not go back to Canada or at least the United States. The detour was unnecessary, many advised me. At that time India was nowhere close to shining. Foreign investments were only a fraction of those in China and the China-India global discourses had not begun yet. The only time India was mentioned in western media was when there was an odd calamity, an earthquake perhaps.

It was a chilly day in October of 2004 when I got this note in my inbox from a close friend from Hong Kong who had moved to Los Angeles. Beyond the expected pleasantries, he told me that the firm had opened up a captive centre in India to support work in North America. He sent me some contacts. I followed up and arranged to meet the head of this operation in Mumbai in December. Walking into the office in Mumbai (which would eventually end up being my future office), I was sure I was again in a time warp – gone were the dilapidated buildings and non-functioning elevators. The office space was slick, modern, connected, people around exuded the same confidence and energy that one would imagine at an office in New York or London or Shanghai – I thought to myself that the time had come.

It was India's time. As a famous Canadian hockey player, Wayne Gretzky used to say when asked why he was so much better than the rest, *"You need to skate to where the puck is going"*. In a business context, the 'puck' was headed to the sub-continent. After a few discussions, I started making plans for starting in India.

At the Mumbai airport, that evening, countless thoughts gripped my mind — I had jumped at an opportunity for a role which was still getting baked. While the office was getting set up, I had moved into a role in which I would run a joint-venture (JV). For those not used to JVs, among other things, they clearly have their shelf lives. The JV was with a listed company in India and hence there would be the added pressures of quarterly reporting. In addition, I had to jump into work, grow teams, make profits, live up to my promise of leveraging Advantage India...

I also had to help my family transition into a new environment and help them find 'home' in India ... in a very different India from the one I had witnessed back in the 70s and 80s. For my wife as well, who had grown up in this land, India in 2005 was an awakening. Something has changed too much and too fast during the last 10 years, she commented.

Confidence and anticipation firmly held in one hand, the sight and sound and 'local' experience at Mumbai airport unruffled a bit of that 'son of the soil' saga. No trolleys in sight, the lady at the immigration desk quite lost at my thick Canadian accent, restrooms had more than the required uniformed attendants sitting idly around leaking toilets .... and then there were the sights of familiar looking crowd (we were no more looking out of place), sounds of animated conversations (could snatch a few words in Hindi and Marathi, suddenly the context of the conversations seemed familiar ... a far cry from those elevators in Hong Kong), enterprising taxi drivers who wanted to whisk you away with those reassuring words – *"My cab is right down the gully"*. As we lugged our oversized baggage out of Sahar Terminal, I knew that at that moment my family needed a lot of reassurance. *"Isn't Mumbai quite like Beijing or Hong Kong?"* – that was the best I could do. *"You gotta be kidding"* was what the three faces were saying staring back at me.

On the ride back to the service apartment (finding a suitable home close to where you work in Mumbai is as impossible as finding authentic *vada pav* outside Dadar, one of the uncles had forewarned me), as I chatted with the enterprising car driver (he wanted to set up a cab agency)..... I knew that I had made the right decision to plunge myself into the promise and perils of India. What the heck! At least I would have some stories to tell afterwards!

The natural instinct for someone from abroad coming into India is that India is quite affordable. Well in fact it is ridiculously affordable ... *for anything with a labour component*, e.g. maids, drivers, cleaners and cooks. However, when it came to your three most significant expenses (taxes, accommodation and transport), the prices in India were on par with the rest of the world. My wake-up call was during the search for a home in Mumbai. I finally shelled out a price way beyond my planned budget and settled for 'Western' prices. Never in my wildest dreams did I think that, this ... that initial purchase would be probably be the best investment in my life based on where Mumbai prices have reached recently ... competing with New York and Hong Kong in some parts of the city. The irony is that many of the buildings look decrepit from the outside but the interiors boast of Baccarat chandeliers and private sky gardens once you get in ... another contrast.

I remember writing back to a University friend who asked me one day on Facebook- *"How would you describe Mumbai?"* I wrote back, *"Well, the penthouse of my apartment building is owned by the son of the builder and he has his Ferrari parked in the basement. Every morning about fifty kids from the slums come and sit around the car waiting for their daily hand out of two pieces of bread and a half a litre of milk."* As I have described to several people, India and Mumbai in particular are an *'orchestra for the senses'*. The sights, smells, sounds ... cannot be found in that combination anywhere in the world.

1.2   Forces At Play – What this storm is all about

When you come out of the storm, you won't be the same person who walked in.

Year 2005 – The services industry in India, into which I landed, was the country's *El Dorado*. We were flaunting our double digit GDP, thanks to the IT/ITeS sector. Life was clearly looking good for those of us who chose to be in this blessed enclave. To top it all, living in Mumbai was like having the cake and the topping, two times over. When I visited Pune, during the weekends, the 'load sheddings' were something 'Indian' and new for all of us. So in a way, my transition to India via Mumbai was a bit deceptive.

One of the indexes of development in this part of the world is the number and brand of luxury cars which are around, albeit struggling in choking traffic and on godforsaken roads. In 2005, the 'luxury car' was the Toyota Camry ... and I remember how when I rented one on a trip to Pune, heads turned as I drove through the lanes in my hometown. Today the Camry is as obsolete as the Yellow Pages.

In the office, I stepped into a new world. It was a plush environment with the latest imported furnishings and technologies. Offices in India, I was told (and sometimes saw), even till the late 80s, comprised of clanking typewriters, telephones with rotary dials, narrow passages, rooms on each side housing 5-15 employees on wooden desks and chairs with piles of whatever they were working on and metal ashtrays. The 'General Manager' had a wooden cubicle somewhere in the middle with a brass (you could get as creative as you wanted) nameplate adorning the shut door. Plenty of peons moving around, and at the stroke of 5 pm... you would find a vacant house.

So when I walked into the Mumbai office, I was not ready for the delight. Hey! this is exactly how the Hong Kong or the Canada office looks like – the new age feeling, more colours, more personal touches (I have seen more wedding photographs displayed at the desk than I desired) ... But beyond the modernized look and feel and coffee machines and potted plants, certain characteristics of the office culture still seemed awkward. A few people would stand out in meetings if they had returned home from abroad, as the 'locals' stayed typically quiet in meetings and functions. The difference in English language capabilities and overall self-confidence was noticeable with a few exceptions. While the practitioners were delivering, taking a deeper dive, you could see that the quality of output needed to improve. It wasn't as if people weren't working hard, in fact they were, but the productivity just wasn't up to par. The missing link, I slowly discovered, was there was no precedence here, no 'been there, done that' moments for these people who had cautiously stepped into a multinational IT setup. The new and very unfamiliar grounds brought with it a certain lack of confidence, though most of them were highly qualified academically. Many were grappling with codes of conduct, diction, attire, and most importantly, values, which came from another country altogether. I have witnessed colleagues who have been in a tricky spot when a women leader from abroad extended a firm handshake. But everyone was learning fast... changing fast. In a public sector setting or even in a local business, the same professional would probably roar!

That 2005 July, after we moved into our apartment, the kids started school and I started to figure out the routine at work, we were hit by a once in a lifetime floods in Mumbai. It was a cruel but ironic backdrop to what was going on in my mind about this perfect storm brewing in India. While there was great suffering in the city, the resilient spirit of Mumbaikars was incredible to witness. It was through those tense couple of days, that I realized that there was something special about this place ... more than I had ever imagined before. I remember how we had nearly 150 professionals sleeping in our offices and suddenly everyone took it on themselves to see that the other person felt comfortable and safe. Cups of *chai* and some goodies from the cafeteria kept everyone going, meeting rooms were innovatively converted into sleeping areas... And amazingly, people still worked. There was an unsaid pact – *"We have a challenge at hand, everyone is in, and our clients who are miles and miles away should in no way get affected"*. One of my first conclusions about India came about that day – the 'blue collar' roots and the resilience in the face of adversity of any kind is what keeps India going in the face of any storm.

The storm forces at play were clear and out – the business environment was chaotic and the talent market could best be described as 'dot-com on steroids'. Talent was all about big dreams. This generation was not shy to discuss their personal financial goals and I could understand exactly what they meant. The workforce was no more interested in being just the 'outsourced', they were fast building their own brand, the return exodus from Silicon Valley continued and we were getting back our batch toppers. In the back drop were interesting juxtapositions – creaky infrastructure and upbeat purchasing power; cumbersome regulations and Indian companies getting a global character; bureaucratic bottlenecks and the emergence of a strong entrepreneurial culture. At the office, around me were fresh-faced hires, who were dabbling in information, responding in real time (mobile phones were becoming affordable though the expensive ones still cost a month's salary) dissatisfied by the *status quo*, maybe a bit of commitment and deep content still developing, but here was a group that could reshape the professional environment in India and potentially the world. They were hungry and eager to navigate this storm. But I was not convinced that they were prepared, nor did I believe that they had the 'tools or guidebooks'.

The Perfect Storm in this context has a variety of factors swirling around to make the journey for these new graduates treacherous but at the same time rewarding … if they can navigate it successfully. Perhaps China went through this churn in the previous decade and other developing countries at the same time, but India is unique given the scale of the demographic dividend, the freedom of voice, the massive English speaking population and frankly, a very unpredictable and increasingly irrelevant government.

Beyond the size and scale of the opportunity, *aka* storm, there are a few factors unique to India that I think will make this journey different.

What now, what next? — Decisions and dilemmas

Caught in the eye of the storm, there are maybe 100 ways to get out of it or none at all.

Today we have what is called 'an excess of possibilities'. I remember my holidays in Pune with my cousins during the late 70s and 80s. Like most families returning to India with a bag full of goodies, we got requests for branded items from duty free shops. They were frankly very modest requests – shampoo, chocolates, cigarettes from the duty free shop, an occasional pair of Levi's for the favourite cousins. One of my uncles stayed in Dadar in Mumbai and he used to say that he could purchase nearly anything that he needed in a 2 km radius from his home. Little did he know about what choices were available outside of his neighbourhood let alone India. The government made sure that foreign goods never reached the shore, with unreasonably high duties and barriers to entry. Today life has changed dramatically and Indians are bombarded with choices of all sorts … from food, (eating *sushi* and *gelato* is no longer an experience …) clothes, to career choices.

One the regular questions that I used to get from graduate classes or new recruits was when to go to business school. The typical response I would get was that "*my parents want me to complete ALL of my education prior to joining a company*". Against this backdrop, professionals are now working right after a bachelors programme and then confidently taking loans to go to business school. Life decisions on marriages are changing as well. And the increasing cosmopolitan nature of the workforce means that inter-caste/regional marriages are becoming more commonplace.

Beyond the various pathways being taken, the end destination and choices are changing dramatically. Should I go to business school? Do I go overseas? Can I become an entrepreneur? Foreign shores had opened up to Indian students and our 'semi-finished' talent. The hegemony of IITs and IIMs is being challenged by competitive higher education institutions, often role modelled on colleges in the West. While insane cut-off grades still rule the roost, the outliers who went on to become television anchors and *sous chefs* (often paid on par or more in comparison to the established professions) were fast becoming a growing breed. So where do you put your bet?

Now with all of this change there are clearly a few constants. Many young Indians want to either be cricketers or Bollywood actors (this inference is backed by great conversations that I have had with several school goers, during a community initiative that our firm takes part in).

However, even if you look carefully at these fields, the landscape has changed dramatically. No longer is getting on the national Indian cricket team the only measure of success for a cricketer. Especially with the introduction of the Indian Premier League, the sheer number of jobs around 'cricket' have grown significantly, e.g. media, sports marketing, specialized trainers, etc. Even Bollywood is broadening its aperture to include computer animation, digital marketing and specialized fashion design. This spells opportunity as well as potential confusion. New career destinations are appearing that never seemed possible only a few years ago.

A colleague of mine used to say that there were three types of people in this world from a career perspective. One small fraction that essentially from the time of their birth knew what they want to do in life. Some of you might be in this category. Lucky for you. A second category that go through life going from one thing to another and then eventually reach retirement. Looking back, they find it difficult to thread together any common themes. While the experiences have been varied, this group rarely reaches significant leadership positions or targets. I would say that this group simply got tossed around in the storm for their entire career. There is a final group that finds a job, and then learns to love what they do. They identify guides, round out their skills and learn to navigate. They put in their hours and many reach the pinnacle of their profession. The challenge for today's demographic dividend crowd is getting out of the second group and staying focussed on moving into the third category. If you are in the first group … I would love to get some counsel.

Everyone is watching you — Social pressures
The forces of winds and water constantly are at play.

Social pressures are significant in India and they will continue to remain so. However, these pressures are changing and evolving rapidly. People are moving for their first jobs outside of their hometown and a new breed of cosmopolitan Indians are emerging. Relationships/marriages are increasingly crossing social, racial, religious, etc. boundaries causing more confusion, anxiety and traffic in uncharted territory. In addition, the economic status of families is changing dramatically every time one person in the family 'lands' a coveted job at a big firm.

My western colleagues would regularly ask why the attrition levels were so high in India. While I tried to describe the 'perfect storm', the one aspect that stood out was the social pressures that kids graduating in India face. It is commonplace that 21 year olds become the primary earner in their families at the very start of their careers. So, when he/she gets an offer that promises a 15-20% increase in compensation, the decision to accept or reject the offer becomes more of a family decision rather than an individual one. So do you go and tell your mom that you are turning down 20% more income for the family just so that you can focus on your longer term career?

One of our tenured staff came to my office and politely said that he needed to *"put down his papers"*. One of the challenges that my seniors had kept on my table was to arrest the high attrition that we were facing (lunch time offers in the next building were pretty common). *"Where can we help?"* I asked him after trying to make him feel comfortable. To my surprise, he said that he was fine at work. His compensation was fine. His projects were excellent. He was learning on the job. I used my 'India' EQ. *"So do you want to move back to your hometown … perhaps to take care of your parents?"* He continued to fidget around and then said, *"It's our company name!"* Huh? Then came a reality check – *"You don't understand! My mother says that I need to get married."* Where was this conversation going really? And then I couldn't resist bringing in some sarcasm – *"We allow married people in our firm."* Now the other side had gathered more courage —*"You do not understand. My mom says that she will not be able to find a suitable wife for me if I continue to work here! Because nobody has ever seen the name of our company ever in newspapers or television. She can barely even pronounce it."* I got to know more family details than needed – how the aunt whose son worked in a more 'known' firm was feeding into mom's dilemma. Needless to say, he left us. I was unwilling to take on the mother. Would have been an unfair fight. I would lose hands down.

I was speaking with my cousin who recently graduated in North America. We went on about how he simply needed to get a job. I kept on taking the conversation towards his parents, peers, anything beyond his job and he gave me a look of – *"Are you even listening!"* The point is that the family is well settled and is not 'dependent' per se on him getting a job.

His starting salary will not be *more* than either of his parents' salaries. His family's lifestyle is not dependent on his success ... only his future success is dependent on his success. While I am not saying that these pressures are negligible, they are frankly not as much as those faced by *Gen Yers* in India.

Clearly I got it — when a 22-23 year old professional gets on his first job here in India, he/she comes with more than just his own dreams and ambition. The family is an indispensable package in the whole deal. More incidents, and the variety of family photographs (the mandatory looking into the camera wedding shots and others) at the work station confirmed my thoughts. Not to mention the packed attendance during annual 'family days' in which our professionals would bring their families into the office.

The social pressures of traversing a very definite success chart (first class, honours, manager title...) make this perfect storm even more unique but I believe that the shift is happening as *Gen Yers* come through organizations. They are chasing success but perhaps not the same definition of it that those ahead of them have in their heads. Theirs is not tied as much to symbols of success (though they do want to make a lot of money).

A person from the west does not completely understand these social pressures unless you spend some time on the ground. "Why are they only interested in 'on-site' opportunities?", a visitor would ask. Well, for one thing, it quadruples their income! If someone from the west were asked to go to India in exchange for quadrupling their income, what would they do? Also, there are social pressures for getting a visa in your passport. It opens those doors which were till then marked as 'Foreign'. It improves one's eligibility in various markets – matrimony, more job prospects, you become the metaphor of success in your extended family, your parents take over your bio data...and life if you allow them to.

A 21 year-old, who starts out at $10K/year is probably already making more than his/her dad's pre-retirement income. At the tender age of 21, he/she is already the primary bread earner in the family for not only the family of four, but also possibly for the extended family including grand-parents and/or in-laws. That additional salary that comes into a household will allow the family to perhaps put a down payment for an apartment, perhaps buy the family's first car or even pay for a domestic vacation. It can change a family's complete lifestyle. I witnessed this change in several colleagues who joined our organization.

In one example, a fellow started at our place as an intern. He told me about his humble family background. His family stayed at a rented home far from the city. Younger sibling still in school. While not a topper out of a name brand engineering college, he had a great work ethic. After a couple of promotions and an on-site opportunity, his told me how his family moved into their own home a bit out of the city but still a home to call their own. Soon there was the first car and upgrades to the family home. Younger sibling finished up his school and was getting ready for a degree. The pride was flowing through him. He clearly was motivated by the money but none the less he was driven and was starving for an environment that valued his abilities beyond his pure academic credentials and class results.

Contrast that to a typical graduate in the west whose first pay cheque will be known to only him/herself. If the parents are lucky, there will be some gifts over during a visit back home. More importantly there are few expectations as the pay cheque is an individual pay cheque not the 'family's pay cheque'.

Going forward, I do not believe that the new millennial require any advice on balancing social pressures and their individualism, the pendulum clearly favours personalized tattoos for this group. Yet they will value the family ties and view life as 'the best of both worlds' where you can balance social pressures and individualism versus going through life in a permanent state of moral confusion. I heard this lesson from a wise lady that I once met in Bangalore. She said, *"If your parents (or someone elder to you, asks you to do something and it really doesn't take a lot out of you, ... just do it"*. Where is the conflict?

Who leads us? A lack of guides and mentors

When in the sea and the storm hits, all eyes turn to the captain.

During my early days in India, I facilitated a course on mentorship for a group of young consultants. Ambitious professionals, many of whom were clearly eyeing a path to personal prosperity ... maybe inspired by those young out of college tech billionaires. In terms of raw intelligence most of them clearly went beyond my expectations, picking up for example software development skills in 4-6 week boot-camps while it took me four years of university to scratch the surface. But in terms of the ubiquitous 'emotional quotient', clearly there was a long and winding journey ahead for them.

The term 'mentor' in the context of the corporate was still as Greek as the origin of the word I guess. *"How many of you have mentors?"* I asked them, convinced that like me they would recall their share of memories about their mentors.

My first mentor, by the way was a partner in the firm and was someone I loved to hate, someone from whom I learnt the best tricks of the trade, someone who showed me my place and told me what I was worth at the same time. It was during my Canada stint, on my third day in the profession, I had my first taste of professional verbal abuse (my seniors convinced me that it was all part of earning the stripes). The mentor essentially told me that I had no clue what a consultant was. In the same vein he pointed out that our client was paying our firm $100 for every productive hour that I put in. And that I better understand my net worth right then. It was a combo lesson about the value of time and value of self.... and I still go back to those notes.

Back to the class, I was happy when several hands went up. It was only after probing a bit more that I realized that many identified their moms, dads, aunts, grandfathers, etc. as their mentors. My mother always tells me to 'follow my heart' and it's relatively common in India for an uncle to soothe your anxiety by chanting 'god clearly has things covered'. These were some examples of mentor counsel that came up in the discussion.

The one lesson I learned during my career was that while I clearly cherished the values that my parents taught me, the days of them 'mentoring me' professionally were diminishing ... I was going to have to choose whom I went to for advice and the type of advice that I would seek from them.

While I also go to my mom and dad on occasion and believe in god, I am not sure that they would be the best guides in critical career decisions. I recall an ad tag line that summed it up nicely ... *you have to be careful whom you ask for advice ... especially your moms.*

Reality is that in 2005, with India having liberalized only a few years earlier, there was a void of mentors. This group did not have the luxury that I had when I started with several people around me with years of experience in the industry. Considering that 40% of India was not born before 1991 (that year being a watershed of sorts for modern India), India was perhaps better poised for reverse mentoring.

1.3   The Corporate Workplace – Move away bare beige walls

It is always the same ocean, but the waves make it fresh and new each time.

Gen Y has taken the workplace by storm. It is as if suddenly a quiet and routine party has been disrupted by a group of outsiders who speak differently, think aloud, question the given, and of course are glued to gadgets. Suddenly the informal and the formal seem to bleed into one another. The workplace has become a petri dish where 2-3 generations need to confluence and flourish side by side. A perfect storm moment.

A campus recruit once asked me if he could go home early in the afternoon as his work was 'done' for the day. I reminded him that he was no more at school and that we have office timings which need to be revered. He gave me one of those *"the world has changed since, dude"* looks. With relatively low attendance levels at many university campuses, and students completing their assignments at coffee shops, I could see where the scepticism was coming from.

Corporates for their part are changing dramatically to provide more freedom and flexibility for the *Gen Yers*. The easy part though is adding more variety to cafeterias, providing more flexible transport options, adding more colour to workspaces. No real disputes there. There are several other grey areas where finding a happy mean becomes a challenge. For example, many corporates are introducing 'casual dress codes' but even there the definition of 'casual' varies. While a decent pair of jeans is fine, torn jeans and flip flops are typically not accepted. While organizations don't need to come up with a primer on how to look polished and professional, those in need of grooming should not take it lightly. A client likes the other side of the table to look confident, and a bit of it comes from dressing for the job.

Incidentally, the Swiss bank dress code includes everything from colour of hair to height of heels to instructions like *"avoid onion and garlic"* at lunch! One Indian guide I read spoke about *"using deodorant lavishly before coming to work"*. Wonder how the *Gen Yers* there are doing?

The nature of work itself has changed as India's need for more knowledge workers grows. Manufacturing is still to take off on the same scale as in China (though that might be a future storm). To become a great knowledge worker in a consulting environment, the ability to read, write and speak English has become paramount. As one of my partners once said, that in our organization, it is not enough that our managers only speak English. They need to speak and understand English at a western university level. The sheer amount of interaction with the outside world has grown exponentially and as this generation continues to balance domain expertise with communications skills, the barriers for what Indians can do will come down dramatically.

The other challenge is around **predictability and accountability** – are they clocking exact hours, did the work from home dates clash with a meaty cricket match, is Facebook their default page, what else are they surfing …very early in my role I made peace with a few things around flexibility and accountability – a) Let them know you trust them b) have difficult conversations if needed c) *Gen Yers* don't mind putting in long hours so long as they can choose those hours, they want to be evaluated on performance not face time.

Work Place – Look at the workplace today… From the dramatic lobbies and cubicles right out of the cartoon strip *Dilbert* which spelt success in the 80s, to the 90s dotcom foosball, pool table informal work environment, today the workplace is wherever they are! When we introduced laptops for all and paid for broadband connections at home, the *Gen Yers* cheered.

Status Quo – They are not fond of top down and are more collaborative. They won't hanker for cushy corner offices to hang their degrees in there. *Gen Yers* are already accustomed to working alongside female leaders and, as more of them reach leadership positions, they will bring in even more *Gen Y* women into the fold.

Network – Hand it over to them, this generation can network in their sleep. We have many clients and senior visitors coming out to India and it amazes me how some of the new recruits have absolutely no issues in asking opening questions and connecting with senior leaders. Though some questions might come across as a bit unprepared, e.g. when a chap asked our visiting

U.S. CEO – *"You look pretty young. How does one become a CEO quickly?"*

Ethics – The other good news is that as India continues to battle its corruption issues and public outrage against fraud and bribery boils over, for the most part, the *Gen Yers* are setting a precedent and clearly want to not only see change happen but are making it happen.

This became apparent to me when we rolled out our corporate ethics programme about six months after I arrived in India. As our training team took them through simple rules of thumb like, 'what would your mother say' or 'what if your actions were presented in tomorrow morning's paper' it did not frankly register as much. But when our chief ethics officer gave his personal mobile number and the hotline number for us to call from India in case we observed any ethics issues, the room sprang to attention. The point is that this generation cares and wants to set a high bar but have been disillusioned by the leadership in India. Now they are witnessing a change. As I keep on saying to our professionals, at least in our organization, you have to let the system work. In all honesty, it works most of the time. Unfortunately, that system is still very raw across India but we are heading in the right direction.

Culture – While change is happening in the corporate environment, on the personal side too, beliefs are evolving, stereotypes challenged. One year, when the family and I went visiting the *'Lal Baug cha Raja'*, the mandatory Ganesh idols in Mumbai, during the Ganesh festival, I tried to find ways to beat the serpentine line – *wasn't there a VIP line*? And then putting me to shame were several 'professional looking' *Gen Yers* standing patiently in the queue to get their glimpse of the almighty. Was this the same crowd that was partying till dawn in our office functions and always looking to buy the latest mobile phones? Confident, and reckless on the one hand and god-fearing and thoughtful on the other?

These are the paradoxes that define the new corporate workplace in India. A fresh hungry crowd trying to navigate through conflicting environments with a limited set of guides and mentors and trying to build up faith that their boat will make it through the storm. India is moving forward, despite the recent economic challenges, and Indian corporates will continue to grow and hire thousands of new recruits each year. The new recruits are trying to balance their goals and ambitions against a rapidly changing environment. I have been lucky to be part of this journey and in a small way have contributed as a guide while learning at the same time. And while I reflect back on the transition that I made from campus to corporate many years ago which I thought was traumatic, I realize that it was probably a piece of cake as compared with those transitions happening in India today. Sometimes I wish that I could make the transition all over again.

This first chapter attempts to both give an insight into the corporate workplace of today as well as get to the 'hearts' and 'minds' of Gen Y who in my view are going to dominate India in the decades to come and propel it to the top. Much of what you have just read has come to me over the years. The blogs that I wrote for an intra-corporate audience were an essential part of developing a realization and understanding of the country of my origin and the people I was working with.

Mumbai, April 2006 –
A year in which we struggled with staff attrition

1)   Gen Y or Gen Whine?

Gen Yer: *"Hi Parag, thanks for meeting me. You know I really like this place but I do not know if my current project is taking me where I need to go."*

Me: *"Well Gen Yer, tell me more."*

Gen Yer: *"Well… you know… I really have big aspirations. I want to be leading big teams. But I feel that I am stagnating in this role. I asked my manager for a change of project ,but he says that the client likes me and that I should continue. He does not understand."*

Me: *"Hmmm, you are doing good work, your client likes you, your reviews are great… you want a roll-off. I must be missing something…. (Thinking to myself) In 20 years, I have never asked for a roll-off in my entire career!"*

(The conversation continues. I continue to listen patiently, knowing how talented the individual is and how with a bit of patience this young man could be a leader in the firm.)

Gen Yer: *(Thinking to himself/herself)* …This guy is old, more than double my age …. He does not get it.

On an average this conversation takes place between me and the 'Diva Generation' 4-5 times a month.

The Gen Yers – the trophy kids, doted on by parents, coveted by markets, the cut–paste-create lot , the impatient and the courageous, sometimes cheeky lot (I remember a young professional observing me carefully in the elevator one of those days when I was running late for everything - "Cool cufflinks, where did you get them from?" I did share with him the details, slightly amused, slightly peeved). They think 'business casual' includes skinny jeans. And they expect the company CEO to listen to their 'brilliant idea'.

I recall another interaction at a town hall... During the Q&A, a Gen Yer asks - "You look pretty young (please note that he is addressing a senior leader). What is the short-cut required to get where you are?" Beyond some general laughter on the floor, I was in fact amazed. Here was a confident young man asking a pretty provocative question without a hesitation in the world. You've got to love that.

Does Generation Y deserve all the attention that they get? This topic is especially relevant for India, given that we have the largest contingent of Gen Yers. Approximately 66 percent of the Indian workforce belongs to those born after 1980 and about 40% of Indians were born after 1991. They *are, fast out numbering the Baby Boomers (the exclusive club of those who carry with them the legacy and burden of authority) and Gen Xers (who are often in self-denial about the siege of the millennial). A baby boomer myself, no wonder, at our employee appreciation day, I feel I am at a college concert!*

And larger questions stare us in the face. What can leadership do to best attract, retain and capture their full value, their immense talent, their infectious energy? Should we play referee? Should we buddy with them? Should we play cheer leader to their every win, their every whim? And again are they really so good, or have we overrated them?

When we started to measure the English competency level of our professionals by level, we found an interesting insight … the most junior resources (Gen Ys freshly out of college) had the same language competencies as the most senior professionals (the elder Gen Xs). It was those Gen Xs in the middle levels who were struggling to keep ahead of the Gen Ys by focussing on those softer management skills, e.g. speaking with clients, delivering difficult messages, structuring consulting programmes etc. It was fascinating to observe.

I must say though that I admire all of our Gen Yers. I find them confident, connected, curious, and increasingly fearless. They feel a sense of entitlement which I don't remember having at the same age. I also envy their networking skills, which I wish I had at the start of my career.

My advice though would be for Gen Yers to see life beyond age 30. I have 20 years of work experience behind me, and the scary thing is that I still have 20 MORE years to go. You can't quit over one bad relationship, a bad rating, a missed promotion milestone date. A career trajectory is not a straight line. Life can't be a thrill ride all the time, you might actually get bored once in a while. You have to get over it and move on.

So, as I try and figure out Gen Yers (and I hope they try and figure me out), I am driving home to my Gen Zers. I try hard to reconcile how my elder son has the 'spunk' to 'network' with some of my office colleagues who come home and at the same time gets bored doing his Algebra, while my eight year old feels nothing about writing a handwritten note to his hero, President Barack Obama.

Oh well! I am looking forward to how the Gen Yers will handle this crowd...

Parents' place at Pune, July 2006 –
Reflecting on what I had gotten myself into coming
back to India

2)   *The Freshmen and the Family*

June and July in India are a time of transitions. A transition from searing heat to welcome rains, a time for school going kids to put away their summer clothes and don their freshly ironed uniforms covered by new raincoats and gum boots, a transition from binging on mangoes to feasting on corn cobs . At our offices too this is a time of change. The 'freshers' (we prefer the term 'new hires' – helps us wean off the college days hangover faster) fill the work stations – there is a significant increase in the average decibel level on the floor. "Don't they know that this is an office and not a mess hall?" -- those are my thoughts on a difficult day.

I recall my first day at work. It was June of 1990 in Canada. There were only a couple of us joining from campus (these days campus hires come in scores). An intimidating office foyer, curious and stand-offish looks from those already around, yet we were sticking out our guts. I think my preparedness came about from the fact that I had got a job in my hometown, my summer internships had given me a dose of 'corporate life' (though every company is different), the economy was stable and most importantly I was joining a well-established firm with senior Partners who were more than willing to guide me through my career. I had clearly set sail on a perfect day.

Fast forward to June 2005, a couple of months into my first job in India as the Managing Director for the office. My recruiting lead walks into my office and asks if I could speak to the campus class ... referred to as CR05. Why not? What better place and time to deliver some gyan about the coveted profession of a consultant, about working globally, and about the long road ahead in this profession and how it was going to be a relatively easy transition from campus to the corporate life, especially in our firm. I kept handy some examples from that day in June years ago.

While walking to the conference room, my colleague told me that after speaking to the candidates, I was to speak to several of the kids' parents who were sitting in the adjoining room. Parents! ... What were they doing here? Did these kids not know that this was an office and not the first day of kindergarten? While I knew that parents were extremely important in the India social environment, recruits bringing their parents to work was a new twist. I promptly had to switch gears and went to meet the parents ... many who looked like my aunts and uncles who probably raised their kids in a middle class environment and then allowed their kids to move out of their hometowns for the first time. Their faces were full of anticipation and anxiety ... in essence they were living the journey from campus to corporate life with their sons and daughters.

First the youngsters — Fielding a series of questions ranging from time to be spent 'on the bench', to whether jeans are allowed and then broader questions about the Indian economy and its dependence on the US and global economies.

Next stop -- the parents! They added questions about safety in Mumbai (kid was moving to Mumbai from a small town on the other side of the country ... their FIRST visit to Mumbai), cafeteria food, whether the kids had to work at home and whether our health insurance covered the parents as well.

Mentally exhausted, it was at that point that I started to get a grasp about what was going on in India. An economy that was roaring ahead, extremely smart kids being thrown into the whirlwind, anxious parents with little background about the profession being pulled along -- several significant transitions happening in parallel.

At that moment, 1990 felt like a walk in the park!

9.30 PM, Mumbai, September 2009 – Having worked through the year-end performance cycle

3) The Slave Driver, the Intellectual, the Army General, the Diplomat and me — Be a Mentor

The whole of last week I have been soaking in 'year-end emotions'. People have been walking in and out of my office – some thank-you notes, some second consultations, some recalibrations, some disappointments. Indeed this can be an emotional time of the year. During one such 'reflection' session, a young practitioner inquired – "Parag, who was your mentor during your early days ….. who guided you through these year-end cycles?" I somewhat translated that into – "It must have been easy for you when you started your career."

June 11, 1990 - My first project. My second day at work. I had five days to complete a feasibility study about whether to lease or buy computers for a client. Those days it was about PCs, local area networks and a printer or two! I thought to myself that this was going to be a snap. A day and a half - that's all it took me to prepare a single sheet of awesome analysis. I reached the Partner's office with quick, confident steps. "What are you doing in this profession?" -- his words tore right through me. He reminded me that my billing rate was $100 per hour – a serious amount that my clients were spending on ME and that I needed to come up with something more than "scribbles on the back of an envelope". A wake-up call. I was clearly depressed. That day I realized that I couldn't do it all by myself... I needed someone, perhaps many *people, who could guide me through this profession, help me understand its 'ups and downs' (though at that time I was only seeing the 'downs'). I needed mentorship.*

If I filter through all of my contacts, four mentors come to mind whom I have leveraged at critical career junctions, making my journey from the classroom to the corporate boardroom a memorable one ..... although a bit of a roller-coaster. I like to refer to them, respectfully, as the Slave Driver, the Intellectual, the Army General and the Diplomat.

The Slave Driver *– He came right at the beginning of my career (the same chap who tore apart my report), helping create the much-needed visibility for me. But he made me work like a dog! He did open doors for me, identified the inroads, was ruthless about sizing me down, pointed to my minuscule errors and then went out of his way to help me figure out the profession.*

The Intellectual *– The Intellectual came into my life when I was just about to ride the 'high wave' of becoming a Senior Consultant. Is it about big money? Telling time on borrowed watches? At such times the Intellectual inspired me (actually woke me up) to "go back to first-principles", reminded me that this profession is not all about 'smoke and mirrors'. At the end of the day you need to create real and tangible value for the client. And for that you need real content, not re-hashed PowerPoints.*

The Army General *– He came at a stage when I was ready to lead a team. Lesson I – FOCUS, be accountable, be war-ready during crisis. Lesson II - everything "always is in the best interest of the unit NOT the individual". Lesson III - stay committed to the leadership decision (whether you* *agree or not!) and NEVER doubt the direction/target to be achieved. Lesson IV - never rest until 'the hill' is taken… and the learnings went on.*

The Diplomat *– This mentor happened to me at a more senior leadership stage. He guided me on how to make my voice heard (thought I am still figuring that out), how to build consensus, how to accommodate different points of view, how to be discreet (sometimes typically 'diplomat poker-faced'), how to choose my battles and sometimes operate below the radar.*

Today, I still reach out to a couple of them, whether I am on the peak of my 'sine curve' or at the trough. They have consistently and genuinely taken an interest in me through the years, given me the fillip when needed. However, while professionally all of them have had a great influence on my life and career, I have never tried to 'totally mimic' any of them, nor (to tell the truth) have I always followed their direct advice… they never expected me to. So, I never hesitate to give them feedback (the tone is humble though). This, I believe, has led them to respect and understand me better professionally, and over time personally. And as the interactions progressed, I have seen myself steadily becoming their peer.

So, as we start a new year, absorb our year-end ratings, set new goals and milestones, understand that many have several decades of professional life ahead of you …….. look out for the Slave Driver or the Army General somewhere around you. Be proactive, nurture, invest and expand these relationships with trust and respect.

As you grow into becoming more adept at navigating your profession, think about this -- the journey really begins with a scribble on the back of an envelope!

January 2005,
Sunday night at home after an exhausting day with
the kids …

4)   *Dog Fight is Here. Are you Ready?*

One Sunday, I woke up to much noise at home. It was the winter solstice festival Makar Sankranti and my sons were to fly kites for the first time in their lives. Their first year in India, and they were doing very well (better than me) in picking up the typically India flurry and flutter. For weeks, kites dominated every conversation in my house, some rehearsals happened in our garden, and that morning it was show time… I knew I had to cut down on extra sleep!

As we headed to the community kite flying venue, eager to get our hands on the selection of kites, spools and sharp string (manjha), I was reminded of another era -- my childhood years in Pune during our visits from Canada. Back then, the harmless activity of kite flying was akin to a 'dogfight' - my cousins and me versus the neighbourhood gang of boys. It called for a lot of strategic planning. Everything from our strengths to their weaknesses was taken into consideration. We would make a crude but special variety of 'manjha' at home by lightly rubbing the sharp edge of a broken bottle along a stretched string. The process was tedious, but it made the 'manjha' super sharp and ready for the kill.

The next stage was buying the kite from an old corner shop which sold everything from plastic mugs to fancy hair oil. And then following the ritual of sticking carefully cut strips of newspaper onto a tail with day-old rice. The knots had to be perfectly aligned to maintain balance. This was a war and our kite was no less than a drone. The night before the battle, I remember how my cousins and I felt like soldiers sleeping in the trenches.

Cut to the present. Our kite was ready for its maiden flight. My boys placed their dream and pride in my hands. I evoked Goddess luck and called for those childhood days to help me at least raise the kite with élan. The wind was fair, and soon our kite began to soar. My sons could hardly contain their delight. They were asking me a million questions -- "Is it going along with the wind? What about gravity? Will we be able to slice the other kites?" At one point, our kite seemed to have crossed the lake and touched the other side of our neighbourhood. I gained instant 'superhero' status with my sons. The trek out was totally worth it.

I believe that the beauty and fun of kite flying is in the competitive spirit. Well, this time, my kids were just thrilled to get the kite in the air. However, it was a different story back then in Pune. The terrace of every building in the neighbourhood would be cramped with boys with a single purpose — to cut your soaring kite. The next few hours, the skies were our battleground and the trees around resembled a burial of lifeless kites — the graveyard of young dreams. Amid the squealing and the rapid instructions of the seniors, our well prepared strategy was implemented. We won more than our share, as expected. I remember the thrill of those dogfights till this day.

There were several lessons here:

Get your tools ready — Innovate on the go. Just like we experimented when tying our strings to attaching long tails to our kites to get the perfect balance, we need to continually refine our methods, accelerators, approaches and in some cases customize them for the conditions.

Know our opponents and clients – Winning in professional services is more than developing the best deck and having the best team. There are several intangible factors that will convince a client to go with one proposal vs another. Relationships, matching the pitch to client needs and sometimes changing the rules can work as well

Sharpen your skills – So it is a bit clichéd but practice does make perfect … or at least it does help. There are no short cuts here. You can sit on the sidelines and complain that those winning 'just got lucky' but a series of wins does not come down to luck.

Formulate our strategy – The sky is full of kites each swerving and moving in different directions, you need to focus to target where to play and how to play. You are not going to win against all of the competitors.

Create the right team – In the early days, I was typically relegated to the person tossing the kite up … 'any dummy can do that'. It was only later that I learned that it too needs a special technique as do consulting projects with generalists and specialists.

Develop the 'killer spirit' – A killer 'commercial' spirit is critical. This does not mean that you drop below ethical lines, but on a level playing field you come out to win.

Whether you soar, or bite the dust, or simply hang somewhere out there.. the worst thing you could do is not try at all.

Cottage in Huntsville, Ontario, Canada, July 2012

5)   *The Tipping Point*

After having lived in Hong Kong, Beijing and Mumbai, I can comfortably call myself a city slicker at heart. In fact most of our family vacations involve finding an apartment in a capital city (Europe is popular with my boys) and exploring the streets, alleys, restaurants and most importantly making sure that we have wireless connectivity throughout the trip – a must for the family and for me as I typically like to sneak in an email or two. With this backdrop, it came as a bit of a googly when my brother (who resides in Canada) arranged for a camping trip in a remote part of Ontario.

Relieved to find running water and some sense of civilization at the cottage, my younger son and I ventured out to the lake and decided to take a little canoe ride. I was clearly there to impress my younger one with my paddling skills (I did grow up in this vast country after all ... the land with the maximum percent of fresh water on the planet ...)

The interesting thing about canoeing is that the driver is in the back seat. So when someone says, "Hey, don't be a back seat driver", make sure that you are not in a canoe. Anyway, my son is thrilled to be out on the water - away from it all, as he peaks over the edge of the canoe to spot some fish. A little wiggle here and another on the other side (I am calmly trying to re-balance myself driving) and then splash! You can all guess what has happened, but the interesting part that I remember is a flash in time when you know there is not getting back! Voila! The quintessential 'tipping point'. A point of no return.

While we were thankful that we had our life vests on, and I worked to try and tip the canoe, that flash, the tipping point was etched in my mind. As we worked away swimming back to shore, to my amazement, my son and his cousins were in fact more excited about the adventure while I was frankly a bit of wreck. This was fun for them, the sheer journey of getting back to shore and probably a memory that they will cherish.

Fast forward to what I am observing in India today, we are clearly at a point of no return. While you can continue to get depressed by the economic news in the press and debate at length about our growth, a new Indian 'normal' has been established. There is momentum, there is energy, there is desire, there is pride and most importantly an expectation that India must make its mark on the world map. While we all know that there will be bumps along the road, we have passed our tipping point and whether we like it or not, India will continue to make its mark in the world.

Sure, the pace of that might vary but this new generation of graduates is likely to enjoy the roller coaster and perhaps navigate from the back seat.

Mumbai, March 2013 –
Sunday morning at a coffee shop across the street

6) *Where have all the leaders gone?*

My elder son came home the other day and told me that he wants to be the President of his students' council. He asked me to help him with his essay that would describe the attributes that would make him a successful leader. While I could think up some characteristics, I probingly asked him to name a few leaders that came to his mind. The names included the usual suspects, Barack Obama, Bill Gates, Steve Jobs ... and then after some digging, names like Gandhi and Nehru. Then he pointedly asks me, aren't you a leader?

Well I thought, yes indeed, I am one such leader and I have a bunch of e-mails that address me as 'a leader' in my company. I get invited to 'leadership forums' and 'leadership conferences'. After a few virtual pats on the back, I asked him to read about the leaders that we have in India today. "Pick up a newspaper, my son!"

A couple of days later he came back to me with a shrug and said, Dad all I read about was how our so called leaders are getting themselves into trouble. He concluded that he clearly did not want to follow their leadership profiles.

I wanted to quickly cover up the disillusionment ... he was only 14 for god's sake… he needed to move ahead with more heroes around him. A few I recalled from a page out of history – the Gandhis and Nehrus … something was not registering. Abdul Kalam yes, and then we debated on why Rooney and Messi should be kept away from the list as of then.

Back in the 70s and 80s our choice of inspirational leaders were few, albeit impressive. When the likes of Ronald Reagan and Mikhail Gorbachev came on the scene, we really saw leaders willing to step out and take courageous decisions. Leaders then were strong and stark, you either followed them or you just kept quiet.

Today, Gen Yers have an opinion and choice about everything …. so with their leader criteria. India right now has quite a catalogue to offer – but nothing is sticking on with this lot. So, an Anna Hazare can spark a following and have a seasonal flavour, but it is not sustained. Religious leaders can whip up a frenzy, but their focus is narrow. India's corporate heavyweights have made loads of money, but their core competence seems to be the ability to navigate Indian bureaucracy. Many of them in fact push the notion of traditional hierarchies even more making the distance between them and the new generation wider and wider. Pick up any newspaper and it does not take long to recognize that it seems like a closed group at the top with the same individuals filling their cabinets with more trophies.

Sadly, the choices of inspirational leaders these days are few. And worse, the so called role models of today cannot even connect with this generation. When you think about servant leadership, blue collared upbringing, empathy and approachability … the names sitting atop of India's political and business elite simply do not come to mind.

Where does Gen Y go to for inspiration? Well you ask them and names like Steve Jobs come to mind. He is one who rolled up his sleeves and was able to turn his dreams and passion into products and ideas that fired every imagination, every pocket, every desk. That's the kind of example the young lot is looking for. Look at his spectrum - from being a dreamy visionary, to a fiery revolutionist, to a ruthless marketer – that's why his name resonates.

I believe that when this new generation starts going to the polls … the traditional parties better watch out. The octogenarian leaders and those who are following in their footsteps, taking Indians for granted, are not going to cut it.

I went back to my son and sat down and asked him what he thought would resonate with his audience for him to win his election. "Dad, I think that I need to tell them that I am just like one of them, and that along with all of them we might leave the school in a better condition." I couldn't have said it better myself. Leadership lessons for us all …

Postscript: The Indian elections have just finished and we seem to have identified a leader who seems to have all the answers for some time now, someone , whom even his critics are having a difficult time in attacking. Is this India's tipping point? All Indians are certainly hoping so.

PART 2

'Working Through' the eye of the storm

I hate storms, but calms undermine my spirits.

2.1 The Storm and the Long Haul

Everyone has their own boat, it's a matter of pulling it out of the sand, and putting it in the water and staying there

It was more than one year since I had made my 'India move'. By now I was comfortable with most things, both at work and otherwise, though one is never fully comfortable *per se* in India. You can only be prepared to respond. The real test was when I could maneuver the serpentine lanes of Pali Hill (driving in Mumbai feels more like a video game ... with only one life!). There are many leadership lessons to be had in the roads of India – how to negotiate space, how to nudge in and make space for yourself, how to push back, how to appear out of nowhere, how to make sharp turns, how to be super flexible around changing lanes etc. Speaking of lanes, I quickly learned that the least respected job in India was of the person who painted the lines on the roads which are rarely respected by any driver. Seriously though, driving in India is a very surreal experience. On my trips back to North America, I was almost bored with the 'car friendly' driving scene back there. During one trip, using my India reflexes I liberally used the horn ('HORN OK yaar'), causing some pretty annoyed reactions from the pedestrians crossing the street. While I had prided myself on my ability to 'switch' between cultures, this 'gift' was clearly being challenged once again.

Meanwhile, my family was totally soaking in 'home ground' – literally 'tasting India' as we went cuisine hopping (what my dad tried to show us about India during those hurricane tours, I almost could do that sitting in a restaurant – "So this is *chole bature* ... comes from Punjab which grows wheat and chickpeas ... while the *idlis* and *dosas* are a staple of the south"). My kids who were absorbing the local culture like sponges quickly started giving me looks that reminded me of my patronizing tone. Their Hindi speaking skills quickly surpassed mine (not a big challenge) which they leveraged to full capacity in movie theatres as they started explaining and interpreting scenes and dialogues to me. I thought to myself that I had 'outsourced' Indian-culture building in my kids by bringing them to India.

Interestingly, foreign foods had started making their mark with fondue and sushi becoming more readily available. One colleague remarked how he could get gelato at the Mumbai airport now ... it was a big milestone for him after settling down in India (frankly, I would take a *malai kulfi* any day). Getting a decent cheesecake was no longer a rarity. What a contrast I thought to the 70's and 80's when the only cheese available was of the canned variety (no idea when it was packaged but opening the cover with innovative kitchen equipment was quite a family occasion at my cousin's). We had family friends who would bring mozzarella from Canada just to make pizzas during their India visits. Sunday brunches in Mumbai were an especially grand affair and as my brother remarked on one of his visits, *"Only in India can you get smoked salmon and sabudana khichdi in the same buffet!"*

Back at office, we were steadily growing in size and reputation. As new cohorts of young professionals joined, I would sometimes get a little nervous whether what we had to offer would match up to the dreams and aspirations they were set against. Here was a high maintenance generation, sheltered from criticism and failure, one who had to prove everything by the age of 30. When we introduced a career customization program to promote work flexibility in which professionals could 'dial-down' their pace of work, several new recruits came to me asking for a 'dial-up' option. *"I want to be a leader in the firm by 30, any quick tips?"*, said one new recruit.

I was impressed by the enthusiasm of one new MBA recruit. He joined our technology practice. After spending a few months in that practice, I could sense that he was looking to land up on Wall Street. He started writing points of views on the banking industry and wanted me to review them with our banking experts in the US. We were able to get him on an assignment overseas for a couple of years. Upon returning, he told me that he thoroughly enjoyed his experience but wanted to do something else. Later he requested for a transfer to another part of our practice, again getting him a step closer to his goals. After facilitating the transfer, a few months later I inquired about how he was doing as he seemed to be doing well. At his invitation, I joined him for a lunch meeting. He told me that he wanted to meet me in person to tell me that he had decided to quit. I listened to the, *"Well Parag, you are my mentor so I wanted to tell you in person ...."*. He told me that he was getting anxious that after six months, he had only got onto a couple of projects and was now being asked to get onto another but this time it was not *exactly* aligned to his future banking goals. How impatient, I thought to myself. I asked, *"What did you want to do?"* He replied, *"Well, I really do not want to do this engagement as it is not in my career plan so I have decided to hand in my papers!"* While I loved his ambition whenever I had a chance to speak with him in the past, if he could manage his patience, I thought to myself, he could be one of those future leaders emerging from the storm that India will desperately need. Two years later, he was calling me up again... *"Parag, any new my kind of opportunities for me?"* Hmmm ... I thought to myself, perhaps this one might end up drifting in the storm through to his retirement.

Once inside this storm the days, weeks, months and years can seem very long. The lull can sometimes be disconcerting. There are stories of sailors who have, when there is no so much as a ripple on the sea, yearned for choppy weathers. And those going through choppy waters yearn for calm. I was having this conversation with one of our new recruits, barely a few months into her role coming to me and saying that she was 'kind of bored' with her current scope of work (*"It is the same things over and over again, I have already learned 'this technology'?"*) I reflected on a conversation with my son as he changed grades and was studying a unit on the Second World War ... again. He came back and said,

"There is nothing new here, why do I need to learn about it again!"

Thinking back, I do not think that I would have dared to have such a conversation with my superior (or my dad) back when I was growing up. The philosophy was more like, dig, work like a dog, earn the respect and the confidence of others in the office and then maybe punch in such a favour.

At 23, I did something like that. My first assignment was nothing dramatic – a feasibility study about whether to lease or buy computers for a client (the whole computer landscape comprised PCs, printers and LAN). I knew one thing – if I needed more action than this, I had to write the acts myself. Act 1 – Dig and Stay put. Act 2 – Chalk the next – for me it was to get a management degree after a couple of years of work. Act 3 – Soliloquy – don't advertise your plans to too many people. Act 4 – Find a mentor cum sponsor. I found mine, actually several. And only after I had housed a few brownie points with him did I ask him for advice – *"I think I am ready for a MBA programme. I want to learn more about the nuts and bolts of business. What do you suggest?"* Now I got him not only coming back with deliberations and details on which universities I should apply to (actually he only suggested one … his alma mater), he also assisted me with my entrance essays, and finally gave me a laptop (they actually had those in the early 90s … though no e-mail or Internet) to use. It was much about right timings, pacing yourself, and laying the building blocks for a long journey … now 23 plus years and going.

Thinking back to my conversations with new recruits at campus, the first stunned look I get is when I tell them that I have stayed with the same company for more than 20 years. I also tell a story about when I started work as an analyst out of university in Canada, my Managing Director came to my desk, shook my hand and said, *"I look forward to you becoming a Partner in this firm in ten years!"* Wow! I recall how I felt a bit nervous and excited all at once at that moment ... but one thing was rock solid, my future goal was set ... to become a Partner in this firm! The pinnacle of the profession. It was not about making it to a Manager-level. As I often remind people, you have to look at the horizon when you walk versus simply staring at your own feet. A career is more like a marathon rather than a sprint as the cliché goes and you might as well 'go for it' as paradoxically while careers run long, life is pretty short.

Working through this marathon, once in a while, when you are not expecting it, you can get hit with a 'wake-up' call and get thrown off course. In a work context that wake-up call is typically a year-end review that leads to a difficult conversation with a manager or supervisor. Reality is that I have been on both sides of these conversations before. In 20 plus years, everyone probably has. The unique environment of the India's perfect storm though creates a sense of, *"this can't be happening to me"*, moments. One of my challenging tasks in my role was to tell people that they had plateaued professionally in our firm, a conversation that is clearly the most difficult part of the job. The reactions that I have witnessed typically end up in a lot of emotional turmoil and in many cases, a pre-mature decision to give up.

In the end, I have tried to explain that *"they were not failures"* but were simply not meeting a very competitive trajectory in the firm – two very different points. By the way, I have kept in touch with many of these professionals and I am happy to say that for the most part they have figured their way out and even landed bigger roles than they had in our organization. I recall a leader back in Canada describing this profession as one *"not for the faint of heart"*. This manager's worry was explaining to his family, parents and the ensuing social stigma that he felt he would have to carry around with him. Somehow failure is more difficult to deal with in India (and probably in Asia more broadly).

When we visited India back in the 70s and 80s, and my cousins were in school, I was amazed at how openly they shared their test/exam results with not just parents but with neighbours and even extended families and friends. Advice was doled out freely and if the report card had happy numbers, it became the centrepiece for the entire family for weeks – every visitor had to give it an obligatory look (similar to wedding photographs). Back in Canada, we never shared our results with others beyond parents (and perhaps not even with parents in the later years), and they were forgotten by the next day.. The pressure in India must have been brutal. Fast forward to today, while some of this pressure is shifting and personal successes and failures are staying at an individual level, broader family expectations still rule and haunt.

The situation is very similar in the far east. I recall when I was in Hong Kong and we decided not to promote a senior consultant. I thought that I could deliver a 'good news / bad news' story ... no promotion but a decent raise as the economy was pretty robust. He came back with, *"Give me the promotion, but I do not need the money!"* Wow! Back in Canada, more money would have been fine and the senior consultant would be running to the bank. Titles were fine, but in fact many people did not even mention them on their business cards – if they even had business cards.

With all this pressure, this generation sometimes tries to balance the need to get short term impact versus working towards the long term goal – a very difficult balancing act in the fury of the perfect storm. As a starting point, this generation needs to understand that careers are not made by 'topping everything that you do' but managing the troughs as well as the peaks. In fact nearly all incredibly successful people will recount how they worked themselves out of a hole as opposed to how they stood first at every stage of their career. Careers are not a straight line up and to the right, but more likely a series of ups and downs, kind of like the stock market or like bouncing around in a storm, and by the way careers last about 80,000 hours!

What also makes this journey in present day India so much more exciting and interesting is that we are on a new course. Great explorers do not fear the unknown. They relish ambiguity, take risks and mine for those opportunities.

The following selection of blogs were written to emphasize the long journey ahead. Many Gen Yers today cannot see beyond their 30s, but it creeps upon them pretty quickly. I have seen many careers flatten or even fizzle out by 40 as keeping up the momentum has been very difficult. Also, in a hyper growth environment, we need to remind ourselves that there are typically deep recessions at least once every ten years and even the India growth story will be hit. Navigating these peaks and troughs will be tricky but at the same time exhilarating. Memories being written along the way.

After visiting relatives at a family function in Pune, August 2009

1.   Life is Short, Careers Run Long

A couple of years ago my uncle passed away. The funeral was a sombre setting for a family reunion but effective. I got a chance to meet relatives, neighbours and friends, many of whom I had lost touch with. It struck me during those pensive moments that they had all grown so much older than what I last remembered. Pretty obvious, you must be thinking, but a wake-up call for me. The small kid whom my cousin and I loved to tease during those summers of the 70's ...... stood there in front of me, all of 39 years.

When did it all change? Too soon? Who set the clock this way? Where did the years slip into? The hard facts about how life is too brief a season drew upon me rather strongly. It preoccupied me well into the night, as I stood there watching the flames at the open-air crematorium. Ironically, while standing there the first row as the final rites took place, I recalled a remark, made in jest, by my brother at the time of my moving back to India six years ago – "You will now have 'front-row seats' to all that is India." That evening I did not want the front-row seat at all.

The chain of thoughts led me to observe that while life sprints ahead uncontrollably, careers are more like a stable marathon. A career can have a longer shelf-time in an otherwise blink-and- gone life. It comprises a good 40 years of our lives (interestingly, most marathons are approximately 42 kilometres!). A career is something that you can bank on, most often control and manage. However, while you have the luxury of making choices about where to take your career next, one thing you need to ask yourself right at the start is – "Do I want to do the 10 second sprint or plan for the long marathon?"

The mental preparation for running long distances and managing a long-term career are very similar. So what are some quick ground rules then for running the marathon? Here are some that come to mind:

- *Understand the full course. Beyond the visible track, take cognizance of the hills and obstacles. Eventually there is a winning line.*
- *Stay on the course regardless of obstacles. Work your way through them. It will pay off. Don't deviate, distractions are costly.*
- *Build up energy, endurance and appetite for long up-hills.*
- *Look for opportunities to expand your horizon and get a better view of the path ahead. Meet new people, learn*

about new ideas, strategies, 'bold plays' and emerging themes. Broaden your aperture.

- *Stay fuelled.* Dive into your energy reservoirs and rejuvenate yourself every now and then. Time them well during the relatively easier down hills.
- *Anticipate 'the wall' well in advance and strategize early for how to get through it. It can be emotionally and physically draining.*
- *Finally, celebrate the wins along the way and remember to capture the journey.*

It is easy to do the long jaunt when we don't do the same things or play the same role forever. We are constantly being challenged to re-invent ourselves, re-examine our goals. We keep searching for the next hill, our finishing line still far, far away.

So, as you get ready for the next lap in your careers – fuel yourself, be alert, be fully engaged and energized, replenish and top up your fluids (competencies), enjoy that mix of fatigue and adrenalin.

Count your blessings that careers come with a long shelf-life while life doesn't consult you much about timings. Finally, remember that in managing your career you have a front-row seat.

Hyderabad Airport, August 2008 – Post another round of year end discussions.

2. Sine Curve Theory

When I reflect on my career graph, I don't see a smooth line, I see twists and turns that are sometimes unmanageable, unimaginable. There are of course some wonderful peaks, admission to the partnership and big wins in the market, when I have been in an overdrive mode. Then, there are the valleys – proposal losses to the competition. I thought that we had the deals in the bag but we were out maneuvered in the end. Very painful. After the pain fades away (it always does), one does get the time to reflect and re-charge.

As a mathematics graduate, I find it easier to relate to the Sine Curve, albeit one that continues to rise over the long term. I am sure your career too displays a similar design. I am never too ecstatic with the peaks and not too blue with the troughs, but just try and make sure that over the long term there is a rising trend. It's just life's way of balancing things out.

Likewise, performance ratings in year-end reviews should be viewed as a measurement in a point in time. There will be a mix of 'exceeding expectations' and simply 'meeting expectations' over a period of time. We all want the former, accept a rating in between, and shun the latter. The latter is perceived as a non-performer or a disappointment. False. A 'meeting expectations' is no less a performer than an 'exceeding expectations'. Given that you are all working with a leading organization, implies that you are all 'exceeding expectations' against an average industry benchmark … a.k.a the middle of the demographic dividend. I believe that 'exceeding' probably got lucky (right place, right project, right timing among other things). They are the ones who have been able to punch above their weight and move ahead.

I must add that a 'not meeting expectations' is a bit of a wake-up call that does require some introspection. It means that one needs to figure out a way to change something and get back into the growth mode.

While, we should chase getting the magical numero uno rating, getting something slightly less does not hurt at all. It is impossible to be at the peak all the time. Like the Sine Curve, your careers will too be a series of these numbers. While you can pop the champagne for the 1s, do revel in the 2s and 3s too and remember that everyone has development needs.

I encourage everyone to reach out to their managers, peers and counsellors (if you have them) regularly for feedback or guidance. Listen actively, do not be defensive. They should help you navigate these ups and downs in your careers as it is likely to be like this over the next several years for India as a whole and for each of you individually.

Airport Lounge in London – Terminal 5, February 2008 – Soaking in the English culture

3.   What's in a Title

To some, it matters.

Sir Paul McCartney and Sir Sean Connery proudly flaunt their titles before their names. The knighthood acknowledges their extraordinary contributions to the entertainment world. It sets them apart from the others. Sir James Crosby and Sir Jeffery Archer are another story.

To others, it should not.

That doesn't mean titles are completely irrelevant. They symbolize the various stages in a career. They mark the milestones in our journey. Interestingly, I have had about eight or nine title changes in my 23 year career in the same firm. While many of the changes were indications that I had moved up the 'corporate ladder' others were lateral moves across our lattice organization structure.

I have worked in a networked lattice organization, in many ways too complicated to explain to friends and families. In fact, titles may not even accurately reflect your role, responsibilities or level of authority on a project. I learnt that early in my career.

While in Hong Kong, I had the opportunity to work on a project for a satellite communications client. I was interacting with senior partners and strategizing a market entry plan for the client. The learning curve was tremendous and exciting. In fact, my then newly minted title 'Manager' did not completely describe my role and responsibilities on the project as I needed to both research the topic and make the final presentation. Most importantly, a 'Senior Consultant' was the overall advisor on the engagement given his deep industry expertise. The organization gave him the opportunity to transcend his official 'title'.

Sure, my ego was bruised, but only for a moment. Soon, I realized it did not make me any less important. In hindsight, it was one of my best projects and I learned a lot. It probably helped me become the overall telecommunications leader for the region several years later. It's amazing what we can achieve by simply changing our outlook.

For most of us, we do not need a title to define who we are – unless we have been invited to the Buckingham Palace. Our roles are not defined by the titles on our business cards. In the end, your work reflects your true value, level of responsibilities and accomplishments, and not your title. Do not be limited by the typical expectations of your title. We need to go beyond.

So, what's in a title depends on your outlook!

After landing in New York, June 2007 – Watched a few movies on the flight … including 'Outsourced'

4.   *Kandinsky and Immersion*

Life, especially now, feels like the Wassily Kandinsky painting in the famed Broadway production of 'Six Degrees of Separation'. I watched the play in New York, years ago.

Titled 'Chaos/Control', the artwork is exceptional as Kandinsky painted on both sides of the single canvas in two radically different styles – one wild and vivid denoting chaos, the other sombre and geometric representing control. During the play, the canvas is rotated repeatedly to mirror the mood of the characters on stage: swaying between chaos and order.

I recognize this feeling. Just when we feel in control, chaos strikes. You go into a free fall. The unpredictability is frightening. Then, amid utter chaos, we find a semblance of order. The conflicts in our environment disappear and harmony returns. Life seems normal, until the next chaos attack.

I have lived through such similar situations, many times especially during my several moves. Moving to Hong Kong was one such experience. My wife and I dove into everything and enjoyed it immensely. We didn't stick to the beaten path of the expats, but wandering 'outside of the traditional swim lanes' … as someone recently remarked was a tad more interesting.

*Experience has taught me of an approach to deal with chaos – **Immersion.** The word, immerse means to thrust or throw into, to soak up, to engage wholly or deeply, or to envelop completely in something. Immersion is the catalyst* *that helps to manage life between chaos and control. It helps us to navigate back to order.*

When I moved to India, it was very chaotic. For me, things were surprisingly unfamiliar as 'my India from the 70s and 80s' was very different from the one that I was experiencing in 2005. Therefore, I immersed myself into the country. This meant relishing vada pavs in Mumbai and biryanis in Hyderabad; recognizing all the Bollywood Khans and Kapoors (Next step: the Telugu film world); celebrating Ganesh festival and Holi; improving my Marathi (Next step: Hindi); understanding where 'silly point' is on a cricket pitch and the notion of a 'googly' and above all, imbibing its indomitable spirit and multi-hued culture. Soon, order replaced chaos.

I believe the way for people to succeed is to immerse themselves into their work. In my university days, it was about getting a job on campus as a disc jockey, trying out as many different activities as possible … from ballroom dancing to skydiving and soaking in the campus life. In Asia, it was all about culture and in particular the food. Whether it was fresh fish markets in Bangkok or 'still live' octopus in Seoul … it was always about the experience and the stories to tell afterwards.

It helps produce the focus and commitment needed to become successful. Not just work, be it playing with your children, dinners with friends or family, indulging in a hobby or starting an exercise regime to get fit, immerse yourself in that activity. You will experience the difference. It brings a new order into your life.

During those initial days I found a friend in Todd Anderson, the loveable hero from the movie 'Outsourced'.

His life is full of chaos the moment he hits India - from the moment he jumps into a crowded train, his suitcase being high jacked into the 'taxi go cart thing' (auto), the ragtag building which is supposed to be his office, he is referred to as 'Mr. Toad' again and again, his frequent stomach upsets, his craving for a cheese burger….

Amid all these madness, he receives the advice that turns his life around: "You need to learn about India". Later in the movie he discloses – "I was resisting India. Once I gave in, I did much better." He not only discovers order, but himself too, during the process. His acceptance of the situation is symbolically depicted in the movie. While the festival of Holi is being celebrated on the street, a coloured and smeared Todd walks towards a pond and immerses himself totally in the waters.

The chaos is unlikely to slow down. Control will be achieved. So, like Todd, choose immersion.

Vishakapatnam, during Leadership offsite,
Janurary 2010

5. *Keep Paddling, Calm Waters Ahead*

Some days are neither simple nor easy. They manage to decelerate, if not stop your otherwise frenzied pace. Everyone has such days.

Our business in India is an enviable growth story as has been the story for many other companies who have invested in India over the past few years. In the last several years, companies have added people, clients, capabilities, a global footprint, as well as physical space. In our organization, we gained experience, became more confident, and deepened our expertise to achieve business maturity. In essence, we've shrunk the ocean, while expanding our global footprint. This means, we have been doing things right and doing the right things.

However, delivering the right outcomes also means making some tough calls. As with other companies, we are also caught in the economic turmoil. We had to make some difficult decisions recently to scale down parts of our practice. It wasn't easy for any of us making the decision, but even more so, it was very hard for the professionals who were affected. Fortunately, we were able to absorb a majority into other parts of the business. Clearly, those better positioned to be re-trained and re-tooled were more easily absorbed. Unfortunately, we couldn't replicate the scenario for every professional in the group.

In truth, we had to align to market realities as other companies have had to do in the current economic storm.

We frankly simply got 'ahead of our skiis'. Companies overall had hired aggressively and then demand quickly declined, and the outlook at this stage is not positive. Please be assured that we went through the decision with careful consideration, planning, and forethought as to its impact on the individual and their future, impact to their clients and projects, and impact to the people – meaning all of you – with whom they worked with every day.

Upon reflection, these times remind me of my whitewater rafting experiences. If you've ever been rafting, you know that it's a team sport. Everybody in the raft has to paddle together, keep focussed, and stay connected; otherwise, the raft will overturn especially in rough waters. This happened to me on my first trip in a raft down the Ottawa river. To secure yourself in the raft, you must wedge your foot into the side of the raft and keep paddling. This is crucial. I realized this after experiencing a water vortex the first time I got flipped into the water. Thank god for my personal floatation device (PFD) a.k.a. life jacket, because despite having one, I barely managed to reach the shore. The time through the metres high rapids, I wedged my foot, dug in, held on and crashed through the waves. It was a scary experience needless to say as at that moment you do not know how long the rough waters will last.

Our journey has not been easy, and it's unlikely to be any easier in the near future. Therefore, I encourage you to wedge your foot to the side of this company raft, stay positive, and be focussed on your work and clients; in other words, keep paddling. We need each other to paddle through these rough waters. Your breadth of skill-sets, knowledge, adaptability, and openness to newer technologies and change are your PFDs.

While, it may be your first time in these conditions, there are others, like myself, who have taken this ride before. And, while I can't tell you that this won't happen again, I can tell you that together, we will make it to calmer waters.

These are waters that I have seen before.

2.2 Sailing Skills – Choose well, stay put, navigate small trips

Red sky by morning, sailor take warning.
Red sky at night, sailor's delight

Choices not sacrifice

When Kiran Bedi visited our office for an event, I made it a point to get a front row seat. An easy orator, she had us hooked and I recall a line she shared, specifically for our women professionals – *"Women make choices, not sacrifices."*

In India, 'sacrifice for family' is a big deal. So, we have stories of how the father sacrificed the 'good life' so that the son could become an engineer, and the son in turn sacrificed his dreams of becoming a theatre artist because he wanted to fructify his father's unfulfilled dreams, and the mother meanwhile sacrificed everything else so that she could stay at home and watch the son become an engineer....and so on.

Well, the point is in this perfect storm that we learn to make some informed choices, and we can ill afford to make them at the 'sacrifice' table. Choices of quitting organizations or continuing on with the same company. Choices of pursuing higher studies or not. Life choices about getting married early or staying single. Choices about leaving India or staying. And if you leave, which country would make more sense. Also, risks are more complex today but at the same time taking risk taking is probably easier.

Thinking back to the 70's, when many like my father made the choice to leave India, the choice was relatively simple as North America was the optimal destination, however, it was a much riskier decision than it is today. One had to take on significant financial and personal risks to make the journey across the oceans.

Life was pretty straight forward in the 70's and 80's. The nature of the opportunities were predictable and the social structures were strong, the rudder firmly in place. Parents would typically advise: finish your studies (engineering, medicine, or nothing), get a 'permanent' job (green card is manna from heaven), and then get married (to the partner of our choice). In addition, start planning for retirement from the day you get your appointment letter – LIC, PF and gratuity would be 'sufficient' to keep you going beyond retirement and in any case, you really do not need that much after you retire as your material needs will diminish dramatically.

Today, the choices are more complex, and non-traditional destinations, typically non-English speaking like China, Japan and Latin America are increasingly becoming hot spots for those who want to leave the roost. The risks, however, are maybe not so endangering – there is a stronger economy in place which can cushion failures. In addition, many multi-national companies are setting up shop and are aggressively looking to build consistency in their employees across the various markets in which they operate. Therefore, while the countries may look very foreign, once inside these companies, work processes and expectations are quite similar.

I was speaking to some university students, a couple of years after I got here, and asked about their plans. The answers were typical, though many more were now leaning towards staying back in India over the longer term. One fellow though put up his hand and said that he was interested in going to China as he thought that it would be great experience. After some dialogue back and forth, he himself asked, *"While the upside is tremendous what could be the downside of the move?"* Looking ahead, the notion of being able to speak Hindi, Mandarin and English in the future would present loads of opportunities. This clearly goes for Spanish, German or French even. As Indians, we clearly have an advantage here given that most who grow up in this country are able to speak at least three languages before they join the workforce.

I was reminded of this in my Mandarin classes in Beijing. There were three of us in the class, a Korean, a British gentleman and me. The instructor looked to the Korean and smiled indicating that it was going to be relatively easy for her. Turning to me, she thought that I would perhaps struggle, but she added that Indians did speak many languages, living in a country which had a variety of languages and dialects. (I started writing the Chinese words in Devanagri script to help with the pronunciation). Turning to the Brit, she just rolled her eyes and wished him good luck.

And speaking of choices and having the guts to make them, I remembered an evening at a star hotel in Bengaluru with a few colleagues in the lounge area and as is typical these days, a lady starts to sing some English tunes ... a pretty decent voice. Regular bar music, I think to myself. My local colleagues start diverting my attention to her and inform me that she used to work for us! Set me thinking - what would one of our former colleagues be doing singing in a 5 star hotel.

I went up to her during one of her breaks, applauded her on her performance and then asked her about how she got there. *"I did my regular computer engineering and really enjoyed working at the company. But I wanted to pursue my musical career, make my own music one day, not Bollywood. I come from a conservative family in Kerala."* Such is the new generation ... confident about alternate career paths, clear about boundaries they can leap, unafraid to dump the beaten path.

Again, an old friend of mine from my Hong Kong days pursued a PhD in Chemistry and joined a pharmaceutical company. Again, a pretty straight path. He then told me that he was studying law. I thought to myself, interesting combination, but given where the health care industry is headed, a combination of chemistry and law makes all the sense in the world with lawsuits around patents coming up all the time.

Navigating today's perfect storm moment requires much more than advice and yearnings from elders. Just out of college (Imagine a 21 year old. Ten years ago he /she was a kid who would probably go off to sleep by 9 PM after watching *Scooby Doo*), and one gets sucked into this storm of choices and offers or the lack of it. The feeling is like that of a boat on its maiden journey that is wind swept and storm tossed. I often imagine how a new hire at our firm feels during the first month – at one level she/he is trying to find decent accommodation, pay bills (still following some parental guidance here perhaps around spending and saving), some need to start learning how to cook and run an household and at work they are eager to present their professional side (picking up jargon, attending boot camps, getting introduced to tools and teams). If you are moving from a small town or village (as many of our new recruits were) to the 'big city', I cannot even imagine the cultural shift. Upon reflection this transition makes my shift from Beijing to Mumbai seems like a breeze.

Then there are those who grew up in the big city itself before getting selected to 'board this ship' of opportunity. While perhaps not as daunting as moving from a village, the contrasts would be just as stark. I recall reading an article of a new IT consultant who was raised in one of the several slums in Mumbai. In fact, he and his family were still living there even after he started his new job. He got into a consulting assignment in Delhi and had to travel up north weekly for his project. He was reflecting on his new life in which he lived in the slums on the weekend and in a starred hotel during the week! Getting fresh linens and maid service during the week and standing at the hand pump waiting for the day's ration of water during the weekends.

Navigate the short trips

An entire sea of water can't sink a ship unless it gets inside the ship

Giving platforms is one thing, having the endurance to push along and make use of the platform is another challenge altogether. Today's *Gen Yers* have a great platform but they have to show the patience of a test cricketer. Unfortunately, many are 'playing test cricket' as if it were a Twenty20 match. Ironically, this is something that today's crowd can learn from the prior generation who showed patience beyond limits.

In India, I also started to appreciate the intricacies of cricket much more. Frankly, there are not many other choices in this part of the world where the sport is 'one more religion'. My first trip to Wankhede stadium was a treat. My son and I set out to be part of history. It was the World Cup final. It was also the first time that we would be taking one of the famous Mumbai local trains. Since coming to India, my boys would always ask me, as they saw the sardine packed serpentine local trains, *"How do you get in and then how do you get out from one of those?"* They both loved the trains in Hong Kong, but then again, those had doors that actually worked! Their efficiency in Hong Kong made travel to work a clockwork-like dream – 15 kilometres in 20 minutes flat. Who needed a Ferrari! Clearly one thing that we miss being in Mumbai.

Going to Wankhede that day, I was, showing off my 'experience' to my son and reminiscing about 'the good ole days' of touring Mumbai in the 70's and 80's, we discovered that the ticket counters at Andheri East, some dilapidated ticket windows, were clearly were not operational. *"So what, let's cross over to Andheri West"*, I led the way, proudly displaying our India blue cricket jerseys. As we emerged out of a housefull over-bridge, we were promptly stopped by the ticket collector—*"Platform tickets?" "Huh?" "We are looking for the ticket counter actually…"*, I said naively. He laughed and said that I needed a ticket to cross platforms. Otherwise, *"How can I tell that you didn't just get down here from the train coming in from Howrah'?"* I replied, *"Do we look like we just spent three days on a train from Kolkata?"* I think my blue jersey led me out of a sticky wicket that day, as my son stood mocking my confidence (Perhaps I had relied on my cousins a bit too much for leading me around Mumbai. Dadar station was in particular very confusing). A new learning for me that day! *Navigating a long journey, means being able to maneuver the short trips along the way.*

While we thoroughly enjoyed the one-day match, especially given that India won, I also developed an appreciation for the traditional five-day test match over the past few years. During those summers in India, my brother and I would quickly get bored of watching those slow, never-ending test matches on television which my uncles and cousins watched with the solemnity of performing a ritual. One-days were more like the baseball we were used to – racy and rushed. During one of those Test matches, where India was mercilessly bashing up the opponent team, I actually felt sorry for the bowler as he looked visibly distraught. And then on the next ball he got a wicket. The energy and the elation that he displayed in just leaping for joy, was amazing to me. How do they keep up their spirits in the hot sun trudging along over by over, ball by ball. After each new over, the captain is again revising the field positioning desperately hoping that he or one of his team mates will make the next catch. The take away for me is that they just have to patiently tell themselves that 'the next ball' *will* be a crucial wicket. The challenge is that you are never sure when that next ball is going to come.

Stay Put

The sea is the same as it has been since before men ever went on it in boats

We have run many professional development programmes in the past few years and while many of them were excellent and great bonding experience, the one that sticks out in my memory is a course delivered in which we were asked to walk bare foot across broken glass and hot coals! While that was fascinating in itself and makes for excellent cocktail conversation, it was another exercise in the programme which really left me thinking. You line up as partners standing opposite each other with a long metal rod (the kind you use in construction sites on which cement is poured) between you wedged into your respective throats. 'The theory' was that together you could bend the rod just by the strength of your throats. (I must admit that I failed on this one as the pain was too much for me to handle). The interesting part was when I realized that had I stayed the course just a few seconds longer ... my partner and I would have bent the bar. (In cricket analogy, taken the next wicket.)

Leaving organizations because of missed promotions, bad year end ratings, or an ugly conversation with a manager (I remember that first week of mine on the job in Canada) might distract you from achieving the longer term goal of navigating the storm. These should be viewed as just irritants along the way, a wave on the bow or perhaps some lightening on the horizon. To get you through the course though requires conversations with peers, colleagues, parents and mentors. The important thing is the dialogue and pushing ahead.

Once in the boat though, everyone has to play their part and more, especially in the high seas. People will get tossed around but in winning teams there will always be back-ups and colleagues that take care of each other when in need. In corporate structures in the 70s and 80s, roles were clearly defined. You knew who your boss was and your promotion path was crystal clear. In the era of the perfect storm, organizations are networked, promotions are both movement upwards and lateral and professionals need a specialization but at the same time need to fill in for others by being generalists when required. It is not acceptable to say that 'it wasn't my fault or responsibility' when you are ploughing through the storm and you see your sailing mates in trouble.

Take Accountability

The pessimist complains about the wind; the optimist expects it to change; the realist adjusts the sails

In today's perfect storm, transformation is taking shape in some industries while others remain stuck in a time warp. I was getting a registration certificate (RC book) for my car and was down at the local RTO. Beyond the flurry of activity, a number of people, the so called RTO 'agents', were busily scurrying around. The process from the outside seemed incredibly complicated but I later found out that it was reasonably simple. Papers flowed from one desk to another with each person responsible for stamping and signing or initializing a copy of the application. Approaching lunch time, one lady decided to go for lunch and the papers just started stacking up ... there was no one there to take up her load. With the bottleneck, everyone else was waiting and the whole process ground to a halt. I asked naively why someone else could not sign on her behalf, and the reply was prompt, *"That's not my job"*. That explained the queues and the frayed tempers.

In today's workplace, while everyone has their own roles, people fill in for others. Work is increasingly done in teams. There is a transformation happening in workplace culture that is adding to the challenges of navigating the storm.

Find the fit

Cruising has two pleasures. One is to go out into wider waters from a sheltered place. The other is to go into a sheltered place from wider waters.

A lot has been written about work-life balance or rather work-life separation. As we enter more complex and connected ecosystems, thanks to tireless technology, smartphones, broadband and dongles for your laptops, the reality is that the quintessential 'banking hours' ceases to be. When I go around office – the break outs, the gym, the X-Box zone, where professionals socialize, grab a bite, make personal calls, makes me realize that *Gen Yers* have made home out of their work place, just as much as their apartments/hostels resembles parts of the office – a work station, the PDA, a mini coffee machine perhaps. For this generation, the work and life element is getting blurred. And yet these *Gen Yers* guard their personal space ferociously. The balance and flexibility is somewhat magically known to them... and best be left at that.

I get asked about my work hours and timings from friends from Canada and I say that I typically put in the 9-10 hours a day but they are not necessarily contiguous hours. Early morning calls, a break to go to the gym or enjoy a cup of tea and the morning newspaper. In the office or off to the airport for a flight. If I am in Mumbai, I am fortunate to live close to the office so I am able to get home for lunch. A few more hours, then try and spend some time with the kids. Evening calls after dinner, and then some reading or television. A complete blur.

The final point on this is that it is okay to turn off the phone in a movie theatre, or unplug on a vacation … life does not fall apart.

This set of blogs is about the need to make choices along the career journey. How one needs to prioritize them and how these choices will define the future. In many cases, your attitude to life and work will determine the choices you make. There are also some insights about having clear accountability in what you do and the challenges that you take up ... always having an image of your final destination.

Los Angeles, July 2007 – Finishing up a work/ vacation trip to southern California

1. Eggs and Oranges?

During one summer in Canada, while at the university, I remember watching Cirque de Soleil (Circus of the Sun). This hippie circus, which originated in the small city of Quebec, rose to become the top cultural exports of Canada alongside Blackberry, ice hockey, and maple syrup. It was still early days for this celebrated modern day circus and it did not have the intricacies that it does now. Yet, I was completely enchanted.

My favourite act at the circus was juggling. I would sit mesmerized, and I must confess that the act inspired me greatly. In fact, it inspired me so much, that every free hour was spent trying to build skills around my new found passion. I figured if those guys could toss 20 colourful balls and devil sticks in the air and keep them from falling, how difficult could three tennis balls be? However, weeks later, and despite an ardent practice schedule (some of which ate into study hours), I couldn't tackle the challenge. A chipped vase, a cracked coffee mug, and a slightly bruised ego later, I gave up the intent.

Recently, I decided to take up juggling again. Well, not because I wanted to run off to the circus, but to bring home a strong point. Here is the situation I was in: I was getting ready to deliver a presentation on priorities and the need to prioritize. I wanted to drive home the point that everyone routinely struggles with personal and professional priorities, and that it is an integral component of our complex modern lives. Remembering that actions speak louder than words, I decided to junk the boring lecture style for some actual juggling.

I chose oranges and eggs over tennis balls to make a point. First, I tossed three oranges in the air. For the next few seconds, I felt like a star; a master juggler. Then, it happened. Two of them dashed to the floor, bruised but intact. My next prop was eggs, and my stardom this time ended before it began! I literally had egg on my face, and on the floor!

Well, the point I was trying to laboriously bring home was—we juggle numerous priorities every day – spouse, parents, kids, work, friends, paying bills . . . . . . the list is endless. We know that we cannot accomplish everything every day, yet we want to throw and catch as many balls as possible, especially in this high growth environment. Because few of us are born master jugglers, we lose control and watch many of them fall to the ground. Often, if we are not careful, what we lose might be an irrecoverable object - just like an egg.

Let me explain. The oranges from my act survived. They were slightly bruised, but perfectly edible. However, the same cannot be said about the eggs. I believe that priorities are like eggs and oranges. There are some items on our 'to do' list that can be parked for a while, even though the procrastination may cause some bruised egos, just like those oranges of mine. But one can deal with that if one sincerely wants to. On the other hand, one needs to act without delay on those things which require careful, immediate and full attention; otherwise the consequences are harsh – like the broken egg. Knowing which ones need to be prioritized and to what level of detail, is really the key to successfully balancing life.

Having said that, this is not an easy act to master. I battle with the oranges and eggs every day. Having breakfast with my sons or attending a conference call? Which is the egg in this case and which one is the orange? There are no right answers as both are important. Still, we need to choose one over the other. Where can I afford a slightly bruised ego? Maybe offer a drive to the favourite ice cream parlour after dinner? The truth is that you have to learn to prioritize; otherwise you will learn some tough lessons - the hard way.

A few years ago, on a trip to India from Hong Kong, I planned to visit my aunt. She was an 'egg' in my priority list. Suddenly, something unforeseen cropped up, and I immediately changed her status to 'orange'. I could always visit her the next time, I thought. After all, aren't families supposed to be understanding? A few months later, she passed away. I realized that I had mistaken an egg for an orange.

So, how do I decide between an egg and orange? Honestly, it's about taking the risk. Juggling means prioritizing the 'must dos', 'the nice to dos', and the 'can do laters'. It means asking yourself, for each task, is this orange or an egg?

For me, the stability of the practice, the brand of my organization, and my family's health are eggs. **Finally, some advice - anniversaries and birthdays (especially your wife's!) are eggs. Make them oranges at your own risk!**

Early Monday morning, Mumbai office, November 2011 - Feeling overwhelmed by a dreadfully busy week ahead

2. Every Day Can't be a Monday

"You need to talk to B", B's manager requested me one day. After five good years at the organization, B had hit a low. He missed work, made feeble excuses, showed little interest in projects or clients, and seemed 'happy' to be on the bench.

We met up for a casual conversation.

His body language spoke volumes. He was slouched over in the chair, his shoulders drooped, looking at his shoes, shiftily at me, and then at the door... in that order. His answers were evasive and the tone indifferent and mildly irritated. He was clearly unhappy. Why did he feel this way? I asked him. He attributed it to Mondayitis. Only in his case, every day was a Monday.

Mondayitis is the feeling we get on a Monday morning, especially after a long weekend. In its extreme form it is termed as 'lunaediesophobia' – the fear of Mondays. We wake up feeling tired, crawl out of bed to get to work, push cups of caffeine into our system, trail behind on our mails, and pray fervently for the day to end. It infects everyone and sometimes is not restricted to just Mondays. Fridays are generally resistant to Mondayitis.

Nonetheless, everyday can't and won't be a Monday, particularly if you enjoy what you do.

Work is an integral part of our life. A quarter of our life is spent at work. Obviously, it has to mean more than just a pay cheque. My attitude towards Mondays sort of hit home during my MBA days in Canada. It was a blistering cold snowy day and as usual I was racing to get to school on a Monday morning – an elective on B2B Marketing. Classes started at 8 am sharp and the anthem was – "Treat these classes as client meetings." Halfway there, catching on my breath, I found several classmates strolling along – did I miss something? Were the classes cancelled? One filled me in – "Why are you running? Everyone will be late today. And it's just an elective, right?" As expected, two-thirds of the class was empty but the lecture started sharp at 8 am. Before getting into the days' lessons, the professor remarked, " I see that only a few of you made it here for 8 am. I respect that. This is the difference that will set you ahead of the pack."

Like you though, Mondayitis strikes me too, sometimes. After all, I cannot always choose my workload, schedules, or responsibilities. Some days are difficult, disappointing, slow, futile, and a never-ending battle. However, I can choose my approach to the situation. The antidote to keep Mondayitis at bay is simple – have an optimistic outlook, a clear sense of direction, a hunger for knowledge and learning, the ability to broaden and deepen your scope of work and responsibilities, a capacity to cope with stress and negativity and, most importantly, have lots of patience, sometimes laugh them off as 'just the way things are'.

Caution note – Even as you consciously keep Mondayitis at bay, you will still experience a few Mondays, but very few.

Hyderabad to Mumbai flight,
July 2011

3.   *Spilt Milk and a Shrug*

One morning, as I walked to the breakfast table, I spotted some spilt milk on the floor. I asked my son who was finishing his cereal, about it. I was also wondering how it had missed my wife's attention. The son looked up from his bowl, gave me his now infamous shrug and said, "I didn't do it." Decoded, what he actually meant was, "Not me, my brother is responsible for the mess. He did it. So, it is not my problem."

While I was sort of getting immune to these "don't kill yourself over me" shrugs of my teenage son, this time it really disturbed me. Did it really matter who caused the mess? He could have simply wiped up the spill anyway. It is his home too.

This episode got me thinking about some of the attitudes that I have witnessed in our offices too. The 'it doesn't concern me' attitude was increasingly creeping into our work environment. I understand we must maintain our focus on our areas of responsibility. Even, our performance management processes award us for staying focused. True that our project, our team, our clients, our challenges and our victories make our world. Anything outside this realm, on many occasions falls into the 'it doesn't concern me' category and is brushed aside with the shrug. Simply put, I am seeing spilled milk increasingly being given a blind eye in the office.

We cannot cocoon ourselves into smug and self-satisfied silos. Our clients are demanding solutions, which cut across capabilities, functions, and even geographies. Our internal *organizational structure (service lines and functions) is of no consequence to them. To win in this game requires cultivating a more collaborative mentality, which rarely happens in silos. Remember, while individual contributions are valuable, superstardom belongs to collaborators.*

A team manager came up to me with a rather unique challenge. One of his direct reportees had a verbal altercation with a colleague over the former's preference of "chillies in food" – the conversation had taken a somewhat racial detour. The manager asked – "Should I stick my neck out or do they as grownups figure it out?" We then decided that if he was in a position to influence then he should go out of his way to have those difficult conversations. End of it – the manager informed me later that things were sorted out amicably after all, and both parties had mutually decided to keep food out of their dialogues! We had wiped up the spilt milk.

In the future, let's try looking out for such incidents and fix them using various approaches. Moreover, when in doubt raise awareness and not just a shrug.

My son's story has an interesting twist. After he wiped up the milk, he put me on an alert. I am now being closely watched for ignoring spilt milk or giving him the 'learnt' shrugs.

JFK Airport, Way back home from New York, July 2011 – Another round of goal setting reflecting back on one of my favourite courses in B-school

4.   Lessons from an Envelope

It was my second year in management school, back home in Canada. One morning, the professor from my Operating Manager session walked into the classroom clutching sheaves of blank papers and envelopes in his arm. While exchanging the customary pleasantries, he distributed the stationery among the students, one sheet, and envelope per student. Everyone, including me, was intrigued.

The professor made a simple, yet unusual request: to write down our goals, and place it in the envelope, which was to be sealed and self-addressed. The submission was next morning. That evening, I sat down, earnestly made multiple drafts, before I was satisfied with my goals.

The professor, while collecting our life's action plans the next day, told us casually that he would mail us our envelopes same date next year.

As scheduled, the letter arrived post a year. Here's some lessons from the envelope:

- *Goals keep us from getting lost* – I wrote "I want to grow into a global professional" … and then set out for a journey eastward.
- *Goals have to be S.M.A.R.T: Specific, Measurable, Achievable, Realistic, and Time bound.* I wrote- "By next three years, I want to be industry proficient in the TMT sector". I

believe, the 'Gen Y' that the majority of you belong to plans for an 18 to 20 month period. So, is that ok – 18 months as opposed to 3 years?

- *Include a stretch goal – For example take the MBA course or enroll for soft skill development programmes. I wrote – "I will find a coach and mentor wherever I am."*

- *Goals have to be personal too. Often, we are busy with our goals for our family, career, finances, and the rest of the world. We forget us. Weave in something for you while making your goal sheet and see the difference. I wrote "I will learn a new language and try my hands at a culinary skill". Mandarin did happen and friends and family are still loyal towards the cup cakes and Italian food. I dish out.*

- *Goals need an action plan. Without it, you will be lost. I wrote – "I will roll my sleeves and get into the business."*

- *Review, Revise – Break down your long-term plan into a few short-term objectives. This will make them easier to review, revise, and achieve. Be flexible to change the course, if needed. I wrote is a s a final caveat in that letter –"I will hit the reset button on my long term goals every six months."*

*I was lucky enough to be planning to go to Hong Kong when I received the envelope. A few others though, were still baking. **And finally a few, well, let's just say, caused me to say to myself, "Did I write that?"***

*Returning on a flight from Hyderabad, February
2013 – Following one of many client visits*

5.   Don't Chase Work-Life Balance – Long Haul, Stay Connected

Patil uncle (name changed) was my uncle's neighbour in Pune in the early 70s. A stocky gentleman with thick glasses, he worked for a bank. He didn't talk to the neighbourhood kids very much … always focussed as he was on keeping to his regular schedule. We maneuvered our throws in such a way so that our cricket balls wouldn't land in his purlieu. I believe that everyone remembers a 'Patil uncle'. His work timings were strictly 10am – 5pm. Every day at 9.30 am, he left for work with the day's newspaper tucked under his arm, worn out tiffin bag clutched tightly. By 5.30 pm, he was back on his balcony listening to the radio, enjoying a cuppa. Then, it was time to debate about governmental policies and everything under the sun with friends in the block. The one thing that was off limits, and never discussed after 5.30 pm was work. His routine probably hardly varied till the day he retired.

Patil uncle is probably no more, and so are those idyllic days when 'work' meant something that male members of a household went to at sharp 9 am and were back home by sundown to carry out the other karmas and dharmas of life.

Professions aren't so simple anymore. Life and work do not seem to be two separate buttons though everyone insists on treating them as such. We've moved on. Reality is also that our profession has become an integral part of our life. In many ways, it defines us. My work defines me. I bought into it that starry eyed day when the managing partner of the firm told me that he wanted to see me as a partner in ten years.

Reality is that Patil uncle's enviable work-life balance is not only unrealistic in the current environment, but a sure-shot recipe for stress and depression, as it's unachievable, but in any profession … with a little focus and planning you can make this work for you and perhaps make it a bit fun for the family as well. One of my more interesting project destinations in Asia was Brunei. The flights back and forth to Hong Kong were not very regular. My wife and I improvised and decided to meet more conveniently in Singapore. It caused less stress for me and ended up being a memorable weekend in the Lion City.

One very stressful occasion was in Taiwan, where I needed to stay back to negotiate a client contract and miss my wedding anniversary. While getting my wife to Taiwan did not work that time, I made the conscious choice.

Here's my take – instead of trying to balance all commitments at any one time, pick the important ones and get those done. I believe that life is about setting priorities and making trade-offs. I have missed family dinners or crucial cricket matches for work or travel commitments. Likewise, I've taken time off to watch my sons' performances at school or simply to play cricket with them.

Finally, I do realize that it cannot always be about work. One needs to unplug too – no tablets or laptops on some days. During recent trips, I put away my gadgets for a couple of weekends. Frankly, my wife threatened to throw them out of the window, so that decision was relatively easy!

*One of those sudden writer's mood days at
Mumbai, 2009*

6.   *When Yes means Maybe*

Do you recall a hugely philosophical and refreshingly buoyant line from the movie 'The Best Exotic Marigold Hotel'? "Everything will be all right in the end... if it's not all right, then it's not yet the end" – Dev Patel as Sonny, the spunky manager of a dilapidated hotel, declares to a set of distraught guests. The latter have this look on their faces –"What does that mean for god's sake?"

The scene flashed before me, a few weeks ago, while I was organizing my son's thread-ceremony. Confident that I could handle those twenty odd vendors (the usual caterers, florists…) with the precision of a consulting old-hand, I got on one of those 'event status' calls. Somewhere, in the backdrop of my psyche, played out those efficient and nimble dabbawallas organizing their routes, transferring goods and employing six sigma quality processes to make sure that all of the milestones were met. Reality check from a sample conversation (literal translation from Marathi) –

Me: So just to remind you, the event is on the 28th.

Vendor: Don't worry. We will be there by noon.

Me: The event is in the morning!

Vendor: We 'should' be able to make it.

Me: Should? Can you confirm?

Vendor: Don't worry. My brother will be there.

Me: Your brother?

Vendor: Yes. He is 'just like a brother' to me. What I know… he knows.

Me: (Starting to worry profoundly now …)

Thankfully, after several of these conversations where my patience, my Marathi vocabulary and my EQ were put to test, the ceremony turned out well.

Reflecting on the event now, and after being on the receiving side of a 'what does it mean for god's sake' dialogue, I wonder whether our clients and colleagues experience such 'left to interpretation and fate' conversations, when interacting with us!

In our profession, authentic and patent communications is critical. Vague 'consulting jargon speak' just won't do. Also, given the virtual nature of our interactions, it is even more pressing that each conversation is conclusive and to the point, leaving both sides with a clear understanding about an agreed set of responsibilities. To me, it begins with 'efficient listening,' insisting (when needed) – "Can you please clarify" or "I do not understand," making sure there is no room for contradictions and guess work.

I recall how once during a recent client visit, one of the visitors enquired – "How many Oracle practitioners do we have here?" Within a span of ten minutes, she received five answers!

We quickly saved the moment and explained how we have Oracle capabilities in five different service lines, and "in the end, it was alright". However, for those few minutes, I felt like a guest checking in at the Exotic Marigold Hotel!

July 2008….
Monsoon afternoon at Mumbai

7.   *That 25 Percent*

Mumbai monsoons always remind me of our campus recruiting season... these months are all about endless travel, hair-raising logistics, cramped auditoriums, standing for hours and making formal presentations about the ' Value Prop'...

For our prospective candidates too, it is a nerve-wrecking time. Tackling those tricky aptitude tests, complex case studies, and probing interviews. So how do you build a bridge with spaghetti? Thinking about it, I am not sure I would have made through our hiring process 22 years ago!

During one such campus visit, I was to address a group of around 300 students, very bright, but clearly worn out by sitting through corporate PPTs. That's when we called an audible and decided to chuck the PPT and simply focus on questions that a typical graduating student would have:

- *What kind of work do I actually start with? Backend? Front end?*
- *What is the growth path?*
- *Do I get a chance to interact with actual clients?*

A few questions from the floor, and then one from a chap sitting in the second row—"Typically, how much time do we have to spend on the bench after joining?"

"During the past four years, how much time have you spent in the classroom versus not?" I retorted.

He informed me that 75% attendance was mandatory. This time I sounded softer, "It's funny how some things stay the same. The utilization target of my team is about 75 percent."

Curious me went on, "So what do you do when you are on the campus 'bench', that is not attending classes?" "Well, I catch up on my sleep!" it was his turn to return volley.

"That 75% is a given. What you do with the remaining 25% is what will define your success in an organization. So don't worry about the bench time, think about what you will do with that time," – that was my parting shot.

Later, I asked several candidates what they did with that 'quarter' of their day. I got a range of responses: play video games, watch movies, 'hang out', play sports, etc.

I have to admit that a majority of the successful candidates were ones that constructively used their bench time – one ran an NGO to help foreign tourists, another took a leadership role in organizing inter-college competitions, a third tutored kids near the campus. These were obviously the smarter ones. They knew that at this stage that I would not look at their grades and coursework. If that were a differentiator, our Talent team could take a breather, simply send for mark-sheets and make offers to the top 20 on the list!

Closer home, our '75 percent' is indeed all about client service. The challenge is really around the remaining 25%. How do you use it to grow and own your careers here?

Here are some choices that come to mind – have lunch with a colleague from another service line, spearhead a team outing, start a social network thread on a new tool that you just heard about, Jam with the Music club here … invite your leader to it, browse through white papers, brainstorm with your best buddy on how to write an eminence paper …be seen, be heard.

And of course, a quick *dekko* **into who posted what on Facebook and who is linked to whom on LinkedIn never killed anyone! So, what is your 25 percent about?**

2.3   The Mettle That Turns The Course – Looking inwards in rapidly changing waters

When people ask me if I were shipwrecked, and could only have one book, what would it be, I always say 'How to Build a Boat'?

As the storm continues to swirl and choices are being made, great sailors remain positive and are able to navigate the waves with ease. A certain confidence starts to develop. Though in the past few years, I have seen this confidence morph into a sense of complacency. *"I have seen these conditions before." "I'll continue to double down on what got me here". "I have figured out this trick, I can go into cruise control now."*

I often counsel professionals asking them to 'Play to your strengths and discover your personal best'. I have worked with incurable optimists *("much before deadline"* kinds), with those who have shown courage when everything seemed underwater *("let's try again"* kinds), the outliers *("chuck the agenda"* kinds)... It is always when the individual strengths are at play that the team comes up with best results.

The workplace of today is unnervingly dynamic – what looked good a couple of years ago loses its relevance today and therefore skills, strategies and relationships needs to be constantly recalibrated. In such times, being aware of what you are best at rather than trying to patch work your weaknesses is perhaps a way to stay up and relevant – that's what I call *"show your good leg"*. Working to get even better at 'what you are best at' is also important given the pace of innovation and change.

Compared to the pace of life and work against that of the 70s and 80s when the boat felt more like a backwaters boat trip gliding through Kerala, the sailing experience in this decade is a rough and ready adventure with many casualties. There is no room for complacency or over-confidence. As a popular book title says, *"What got you here will not get you there"*. The challenging part now, is that the 'there' is unknown as very few people have reached that destination, especially those who can offer up some wisdom. Corporates in India are trying to figure out the waters and where they will lead. They are asking, 'What is possible with the talent in India?'

This does require taking some risks, taking accountability for your own piece of work, finding the gaps, negotiating, and pushing the envelope.

As I spent more time on the ground, I realized that this appetite for taking on risk was also changing. The new *Gen Yers*, spurred by the momentum of the broader economy and dot-com millionaires, were clearly more open to taking such gambles. I remember a conversation with one young colleague who was doing very well at work and one would think that he was only cut out to be a consultant and nothing else. One day he confided in me – *"I want to start something of my own, and not do this every day."* His friends had been planning a business start-up for a while and he was figuring out whether to jump in or not. I asked whether he had consulted mentors, family or friends. He said that he did not come from a 'business family' and hence he could not really have a constructive conversation with anyone that he knew personally. After a few questions back and forth, we agreed that taking that risk was the right thing for him to do.

On campuses as well, I see a lot more interest in entrepreneurship as even colleges and universities have started promoting innovation. This tide coupled with the increased money flowing into India through venture capitalists and private equity funds, will certainly drive more risk taking. Again, this is very different from the 70s and 80s where taking such risks was shunned and money was simply not there. If someone happened to do something off-the-beaten track, they were viewed as someone who did not do well in school.

More importantly, it's about being resilient after taking the plunge to deal with the ups and downs. While India weathered the recent economic crisis better than most countries, it too was a wakeup call.

In another case, one of our managers took the risk of joining a business, got slammed by the economic crisis, and returned to work for us. As opposed to regretting the decision, he actually had so many stories to tell that we actually started reaching out to him to listen to more of his story. He still maintains that despite the financial impact, it was one of the best decisions that he had taken. With *Gen Y* around, entrepreneurship in India will no longer be a road taken by the one off. It will become a way of doing work, and is just the thing that India needs today. Regardless of where they work, *Gen Yers* will want every experience to feel like a 'start-up' and organizations will need to create an environment that promotes some level of risk taking.

This transition will drive a significant change at the workplace, in Indian homes, especially those who have not promoted a business and have little or no risk taking background. But in India, it starts from the beginning among the middle classes where many kids are over protected from the start. While these parents like to talk about successful entrepreneurs globally, including Indians who made their millions in Silicon Valley, they sometimes miss the point that all of these hugely successful entrepreneurs were in fact unsuccessful entrepreneurs at some point in their lives.

I am seeing that transition closer to home as well among my extended relatives, with a few, 'off the beaten track' ones, who may not have done well at school, being supported by parents in starting off new successful businesses. It is great to see and adds to the changing landscape of the storm.

One of the pleasures that I have learned after coming to India is reading the morning paper over a nice hot cup of tea. In Canada, the mornings were not about having your personal time, it was more about jumping into the shower, downing a bowl of cereal, and getting out of the house as fast as possible. The commutes were long and reading the newspaper was mostly done over lunch, in car (when I did not have to drive, of course) or in the evenings. Mornings in India start early, and once the kids are off to school by 7 am, you can enjoy that time (between conference calls to the US, in my case). When one scans the broader headlines, one sees a common trend of some pretty depressing headlines. A scandal here, a robbery or suicide there and if the markets and the Indian cricket team are not doing well ... then it's page to page depression ... until you hit that one column hidden away somewhere which talks about India making its mark on the world stage.

One day, I saw a headline that read that India was about to become one of the world's largest beef exporters. Beef exports? From India? Well, it is actually buffalo meat (I found out after googling), but regardless, that shows how despite the historic bureaucratic challenges, some businesses seem to be figuring out how to flourish in this environment. I then ask myself, what if these challenges went away? In fact, if Indian business models are able to survive and thrive in this environment, what would India look like? What could these businesses do globally? Well, that is the silver lining vision that this generation is holding on to, and frankly based on my experience, that cynicism about the future is disappearing fast amongst this crowd, unlike the previous one. While perhaps not a full 'Arab Spring', but change is happening.

I have witnessed this optimism on many occasions in the past few years. This is very different from when I used to visit India in the 70s and 80s. Back then, one of 'my tests' when we visited was to speak my native Marathi with my grandfather. He was a towering man with a deep dark complexion, pretty fit for his age. He had a regular routine that included getting warm water in a mug for his morning shave, some basic exercise that included regular walks and even some bicep curls, reading the morning paper every day and listening to his radio placed on a ledge high up on the wall. I always thought that he would have done extremely well in the army! He was incredibly disciplined.

While I invariably failed in my language skills and was not up to his mark on most occasions, this was a great opportunity to spend time with him. In those days though, many of the conversations veered towards the standard politics and corruption that was and unfortunately still haunts India today. How the common Indian had little chance to escape from the cycle. He recognized that we had 'escaped' by emigrating to Canada, but life for the common Indian was extremely difficult. The conversations continued as we both got older. I continued coming back to India after completing my university degree but unfortunately he passed away before I actually moved to India. As I reflect back (and doing a bit of research), the dialogues bordered on Malthusian philosophies and acceptance of the Hindu rate of growth. I always asked myself whether he felt that he had gotten what he wanted from all of his efforts. Life was tough indeed with few opportunities and no escape hatch. Speaking with him though still remains one of my fondest memories of visiting India.

This slice of India is changing now. While corruption in politics clearly persists, what impresses me every morning when I pick up the paper is that many of these issues are being discussed openly. Common people are having their say. The next generation is lapping this up. They are talking about it on social media and you can sense that there is a tide that is building up. And many new *Gen Yers* will be taking risks to lead from the front because of natural curiosity, national pride and simply because they want change to happen and they want it to happen quickly. *Gen Yers* want to connect with political and corporate leaders. They want to narrow the divide and today's leadership has to be prepared to listen and respond.

Living in Mumbai, one gets quickly drawn into watching movies. It is like if you miss a hit in the theatres across a couple of weeks, then you are completely out of the crowd. While my Hindi is very rudimentary, I still make an effort to go out with the family. I typically bug them about explaining a joke or some dialogue. My kids love it when I ask them to translate. (An instance of situational leadership for them to provide answers to me – but more on that in the last section) For someone who grew up in a country that was not really that patriotic, for example, no one plays the national anthem in theatres or even displays the Canadian flag in front of their homes (unlike homes south of the Canadian border) it's pretty impactful to see Indians standing up for the national anthem at the start of every movie. My family and I are getting into this patriotism as well. Beyond standing up in movie theatres, my younger one is the first one to wake up every 26th of January and make sure that we all stand up at home during the Republic Day parade.

This next generation has the weight of the nation on their shoulders. The difference is they carry it easily, no fuss. They were born at the right time and the right place in modern Indian history. They are passionate about the nation as well and many of them want to make India their home in the long term.

The demographic dividend is unique to India and is at a scale that is unlikely to be seen for the next hundred years. *Gen Yers* are doing their bit but they both need to work the daily routines, take the risks and patiently move forward.

With the wind at their sails, this crowd will need to become battle ready to work through the storm. There are successful examples all around them and there is a lot of momentum as well.

This next set of blogs talks about some themes required to navigate through the storm: risk-taking nature, resilience, unlimited curiosity, ability to dialogue, not always asking for permission and finally taking ownership of whatever you produce. All of these themes will be critical as you navigate through your career separating those who simply survive from the ones that thrive.

Delhi Airport, July 2012
– Finished reading Chetan Bhagat's book

1.   Find the Gap and Take the Lunge

A CEO I admire is an avid mountain biker. He once talked about how when you were coming fast down a hill on a rough trail, with a big tree in the middle of the trail, and if you were just focussing on that 'Tree' - you were sure to ride right into it! Well, in mountain biking jargon, it is called 'target fixation'. The obvious cure is not to look at the obstacle but find the gaps and focus on the narrow paths you want your wheels to take. So, here is a sport that requires lot of maneuvering around obstacles, jumping off, balancing, spinning - basically negotiating one's way around a 'you-never-know-what-next' path .... typically at high speeds (if you lose the speed element, it's kind of like driving on Mumbai roads!).

I recalled the theory, when I read Chetan Bhagat's Two States. On the face of it, it looks to be a simple Indian tale of a boy from the North in love with a girl from the South. Clichéd? Not anymore, since it is now used in India B-schools as a case in negotiation analysis.

The story is an exemplary lesson on how to focus away from those obstacles that are in plain sight. It's about finding the gaps, addressing the aberrations, moving away from inbuilt perceptions/ stereotypes, building trust and consensus over time, sometimes doing the high-stake crucial conversations, sometimes through mellow sweet- talk ……… And finally cracking the deal by taking some risks and making the lunge. The book ends with the marriage being blessed by both sets of parents, who till the last moment were 'Tree' personified.

So, here is my take – whether you are in a relationship, a partnership or in a team ….. as you perfect the techniques of negotiating the gaps, you will find yourself gaining momentum with less stress. It will not be easy, it will take effort and sustained passion for it to become second nature. But it will be worth it. Your comfort zone will have expanded and you will be on your way to becoming a true mountain bike master.

As you do the mountain bike ride, downhill or uphill – with time, and with the heady mix of practice, persistence and passion, you will soon be ready for 'the lunge' (By the way, the lunge is a very useful mountain bike trick for getting over big obstacles. It helps get the back-wheel over large rocks or logs). The visual of the 'Tree' will become a thing of past.

Onboard American Airlines, October 2012 – Flying from New York to Dallas

2.   *The Bamboo that Bends*

I write this note, aboard an American Airlines flight from New York to Dallas. I am amazed at the new in-flight internet service. Just a few weeks ago, AMR Corp, the parent company to American Airlines went bankrupt. And here they come up with something to enhance customer experience, though the meals, if any, leave a bit to be desired!

I am now confident that AA will re-emerge from bankruptcy and continue 'doing what they do best'. The 'Resilience' of this country amazes me.

Americans sure have a way of bouncing back. While still not out of the woods, people here have generally adapted themselves well, over time, to the stressful conditions of a roller-coaster economy. And there are signs of economic recovery too. GM, AIG and Citibank are back making profits. Even Lehman officially re-emerged from bankruptcy a few weeks ago, albeit paying back what they could to their creditors. Some of this 'Resilience' is evidenced in India as well. I have personally witnessed this after the 2005 Mumbai floods and the 2008 terrorist attack on Mumbai – next morning it was business as usual in India's financial capital.

What helps some people 'bounce back' after adversity strikes, while others feel overwhelmed and spiral into despair? How do some individuals and organizations manage not to tailspin during trying times? Even, on a regular day, how do we manage to bounce back after a deliverable gets rejected, *when we feel we deserve a pat on the back but don't get one, when the promotion is handed out to the least deserving individual, and so on?*

I recall the time when I was working on my first proposal. I thought that I had produced a stellar work product .... and then we ended up in second place and lost the deal. I had my first real 'session' with the lead Partner and he quickly pointed out that my document was 'mediocre'. Mediocre! Yes, average .... very average. After sulking for a few days and regretting that I had moved to Hong Kong from my comfort zone in Canada, I decided to dig in and elevate my game. Honestly, I avoided him for a few days, until I got to know later that during a conversation with my wife, he had remarked that I was doing an incredible job. Hmmm... I sprinted back into action.

In a private moment, he told me later that – "You should not worry when I am 'yelling' at you... You should start worrying when I stop speaking with you. Giving you feedback means that I actually care about you and your career."

So, in my mind, some of the 'inbuilt springs' that enable the 'Resilient ones' bounce back are:

- *They are self-renewing – They are ready to heal themselves, pick up the pieces and come back stronger. Think J K Rowling. A former secretary, who was fired while trying to type a story on the computer during office hours, she used her severance pay to fund her first book.*

- *They are the incurable optimists – They are ready again to take the leap of faith. Think Ratan Tata. Three weeks after the attack, the Taj Hotel re-opened its doors to guests.*

- *They are innovative in times of adversity – Resilient people have an uncanny ability to improvise and imagine possibilities where others are confounded. Think Apple. At a time when the music player and phone industries were merely supplying standard products, Apple came up with this radical and beautiful product…. the iPod.*

- *They accept and don't get into a "how- did-we-get-into-this-mess" analysis – Think Michael Jordan. After a gambling controversy, he said, "Yeah, I've gotten myself into situations where I would not walk away and I've pushed the envelope". And then his famous "I am back" return to NBA.*

- *They develop a support system – At home, among friends and colleagues, they accept help and help others when they need it. Think Indian family business houses. Think your families and friends.*

- *They are ready to script a fresh page – They learn from mistakes and are ready to rewrite the script. A Phoenix of sorts, they learn from feedback. Think Bajaj who missed the 'motorcycle' train but are climbing back.*

- *Most importantly, Think about YOU ….. the next time you fall down, remember you can stumble only if you are moving ….. so just get back up and spring back into action. **A Japanese saying goes –'The bamboo that bends is stronger than the oak that resists'.***

Munnar, April 2009
– Vacationing with family

3. *Rugby and the Good Leg*

"I am done with football," my ten-year old declares, dashing into the house from school. "The boys play too rough." He has a gash on the knee to exhibit, and an explanation at hand – "I fell down while tackling the ball, and they kept attacking my wounded knee."

After some reasoning, and reminding him that his life's religion was to play for Man U/Chelsea (till that morning), I tell him about a rugby strategy that could come handy on the play-ground…and in life.

An old friend of mine once told me that rugby players often put the athletic tape or bandage on the 'good leg' rather than the injured one. This is a proven tactic to draw attention to the 'tough' one, while keeping the 'vulnerable' spot safe till it heals.

Back at our workplace (and away), all of us thrive in an extremely fast-paced and sometimes hostile playing-field. Be it part of a competitive client pursuit, meeting with a HR person to discuss those dreaded development needs, or simply during project team touch-points ….. every dribble, every pass, every ruck, can make or miss the goalpost. The reality is that competitors wait for us to fail – that's the hard truth. And so in the business model that we are in, we stand to win when we draw attention to our bright spots versus blind. I am not advocating that we disguise our blind spots, or confuse the other side, or position our weakness as strengths – NO. I would simply rally around our share of strengths as opposed to what's not working; find the door and not hit the wall.

A little challenging, I must admit considering how obsessed we all are about weak spots, failings, the proverbial glass half-empty perspective. As an indicator, look at what's making front-page noise around the world – another recession round the next corner, surely the new government will take a sharp detour, IPL matches are all fixed, Cannes fashion faux pax …. Mornings are half-hearted till you hit a few nosedives.

Here is a strategy that often works for me – divert the attention of the competition to the resilience points, to the foundations of our personal brand as opposed to areas of under development. And then surround ourselves with people who have complementary strengths.

So, like in a game of Rugby, whether playing in the Forward pack or the Backs, whether doing the line-up or the scrum, let's just focus on showing off our 'good leg' and get into the game. That way we make it to the 'League'.

At home in Mumbai, September 2013
– Family and kids out in the afternoon ...

4.   *Will we really go through the clouds?*

Some forty years ago, two boys aged eight and four, in their newly stitched formal suits, thrilled to bits, boarded a Swiss Air flight from Mumbai to Toronto. Their life's first flight...

The two boys were my brother and me.

Reason for this flashback? Last week, on a morning flight to Hyderabad, sitting across the aisle from me were two little boys in their Sunday best, obviously flying for the first time. While the other passengers, me included, were in our typical 7am inflight mood, pulling out briefcases and newspapers, fiddling with our mobiles, these two kids were busy otherwise. Window shutters went up and down, safety manuals flung out, seat-belts went through a minute inspection. Also followed innumerable questions – Will we really go through the clouds? What are these buttons up here for? Can we meet the pilot? To my pleasant surprise, a nearby stewardess patiently responded that it was possible, post-landing. More squeals.

Frankly, I could have done with a little less distraction, as I tried to immerse myself into pending emails. But my attention kept going back to the duo – reminding me of that long-ago Mumbai-Toronto journey. Also reminding me how we adults approach everything, from careers to personal lives, from the same 'have been there done that' perspective. As we grow, we lose the sense of 'novelty'.

Back at work, our results as well as the overall economy has been thriving. Very comforting … until one visiting client remarked, "You guys are running a factory out here!" While I appreciated the compliment (I imagine a slick running high-tech plant churning out the latest smartphones), it also made me cringe a bit. Do we really want to be perceived like that ….impersonal, lack of customization, predictable? Can we resurrect the novelty factor into our engagement with clients (while at the same time balancing the factory-like consistency and quality of our delivery engine)?

Maybe we should do more of that "kids in the airplane" act. During those oft-repetitive client presentations – create your own 'new' (re-visit that beaten power-point … simplify, use more visuals). Recently, when we used iPads and personalized information packets during a client presentation, it made an immediate connect. Like those kids, display childlike curiosity, ask as many questions without the fear of being labelled ignorant. Explore new areas versus re-packaging existing solutions (you never know what lurks in the simplest of places).

A final caveat – If you can't imagine, you can't create. So, let your imagination take over some times. Will we really go through the clouds is a good place to begin. Sometimes childlike imagination transforms an average interaction into a superhero conversation…like when the two kids finally met the pilot – "Can you land on water?" I didn't quite stay to catch the response

Bengaluru Airport, February 2013 – Following an executive visit by the US Consulting CEO

5.   *Chuck the Agenda and Say Hello*

During a conversation with our U.S CEO, while he was visiting the India offices, I started to take him through his official agenda – a neat print-out with a high-level schedule – when he suddenly asked, "Tell me something more about Bangalore." Caught a bit off-guard, I began to draw the usual Silicon Valley parallels… and then the conversation meandered into the city's infrastructure (more lack of it), Indian politics, talent market, IPL matches... and then more effortlessly flowed into food, family and festivals. I also informed him that the city is officially called Bengaluru now!

*In a world where we seem to have a fetish for organizing virtually everything around us, that day I realized one thing – the best conversations with my colleagues and seniors (especially those who made visits from other countries) were those which did **not** have a pre-determined agenda; those that were rather impromptu; those where we simply chatted intelligently about our firm, clients, our people, about the economy and the elections; those where we shared the fine print about our country and culture (Bollywood included); those where we helped them see things in the Indian context.*

Conversations clicked when we did not offer up close-ended questions like "So do you like Indian food"? (Obviously no one would say, "I am allergic to Biryani," while visiting India); when we did not dwell on the glass half-empty scenarios and bring up expected 'operational issues'; those, after which, our clients and our visitors remarked how energized they felt.

Clearly, the visiting leader wanted to connect more with us through numerous small and simple conversations.

More and more I now believe in the power of continued conversations. Look at this –

- *Conversations are more energizing because unlike a formal meeting, they tend not to predict outcomes or drive solutions*
- *Conversations allow both sides to be more engaging and empathetic to each other. Both sides listen*
- *Conversations are more democratic versus an 'across the table', and hence people explore issues, invent solutions, and find ways forward*
- *And above all they help to build durable relationships, so that when you require, you have the connections in place*

The same hold true for feedbacks and reviews. For those who wait until mid-year and year-end to book a formal agenda-driven meeting with their counsellor, it probably is not such a great idea!

HR discussions need not be an annual psychotherapy session; they can be spread across "water-cooler conversations" throughout the year. I am not suggesting in any way that we take away the stature of focussed and formal meetings – they are clearly required in any business… but small talk can lead to big wins, and can spare us surprises at year end.

Finally, I am always eager to understand from the visitors about their moment of 'maximum impression', during their India trip. They always recall an interesting conversation or two that stayed on with them. Can't remember anyone who ever got thrilled about a power point!

*Sunday afternoon at the club, February 2010 –
Following a round of golf*

6. *To Sign the Chit or Not To*

At one point there was a lot of improvement in my son's tennis shots and golf swings. I had been travelling a great deal those few months and I found out that he had been going to the club on his own and getting some additional practice. Happy as I was, that he now plays several shots rather well, in both the sports, I also had mixed feelings seeing him calling shots of other kinds as well (i.e., making decisions on his own). I discovered that he was actually signing off the chit (bill) for his fresh lime soda and sandwich at the club after a round of practice! (This came to my notice, unexpectedly, when I got the monthly bill).

Now, I don't remember much about being 13, but imagining this level of 'empowerment'—to be able to go to the club, organize a caddy, and sign off a bill – surely inspires me (also makes me a tad nervous and perhaps a bit envious, as I did not have such freedom growing up!).

But yes, somewhere, I am PROUD... that he had the mettle to do it... to stretch his limits of entitlement... to jump the gun. Having said that, thank god, until date, I only have to foot bills for his favourite snacks.

So, how does all this relate to our work? Well, last week, I asked a couple of colleagues, "What is the most important decision that you can make WITHOUT getting approvals from your reporting manager?" Deathly silence... some amused faces... some deep-thinking brows. One volunteered that his *ability to take autonomous calls on things had actually seen a dip recently.*

In my experience, this is common across companies and businesses. While they progress on many fronts, they still remain more of a culture of "asking for permission versus taking charge". Now, if we want people to be leaders and not followers, and if leaders are to be measured by the number of leaders that they develop versus the number of followers that they demand … then we need to break out of this 'approval gathering' mindset.

Here, many of you might say that it is the leaders who need to drive the mindset change, and who would dare to cross their safety nets and jeopardize a career. Aren't those decisions referred to as CLMs (a.k.a career limiting moves!)? Wouldn't it make more sense to just toe the line, get the necessary approvals from a reporting manager and then make the commitment? Better to be 'safe' than sorry?

Well, I would argue that the change needs to be driven both ways...

My ask of the leaders is –

- *Let go of that safety net once in a while – No risk, no great ideas. You can't play referee forever. Instead, help others understand the choices they have.*
- *Think of a trampoline – Your role here is to propel others ahead and support an empowered, decision-making environment. The bounces and highs are empowering for your people.*
- *Don't let go of initiators and those pioneers who may occasionally take risk – Let them thrive, let them take a call*

..… *if they make mistakes, step up as required and help them deal being caught between the rock and a hard place.*

- *Walk the talk – Mean it. When you say "do your own thing", let it not be "do your own thing the way I want it.*

  To the future leaders, I want to put across this:

- *With empowerment comes big responsibility – Know how to be personally accountable, otherwise empowerment can turn into a challenge*

- *Have the right reasons to jump the line – Empowerment is not a cure-all. So, don't evoke it needlessly.*

- *Own up for any transgression that might have occurred. Go say that sorry. It really helps.*

- *Then …Go ahead and sign that chit...*

Mumbai, February 2011 – Returned home after an overseas trip

7.   *Do you have an expensive signature?*

For a while, I turned over-zealous about my parental duties (usually happens when I come back from long trips) – checking homework status, re-setting ground rules about iPad time etc. After the usual family banter, my elder one asked me to sign his diary, to confirm that he had finished his homework – a new 'control process' introduced at school while I was out of town. Naturally, I said, "Let me see your homework first." He comes back with, "Man, you have an expensive signature! My friends have it easier."

Pretty interesting I thought, if you can overlook that trace of audacity in the comment. As a father, I do hope that over the years, I have earned his respect about 'possessing' an expensive signature. Growing up, I always admired my dad's consistent and hallmark signature, though getting it was honestly easier.

Based on my son's one-liner alone, which momentarily helped validate my ego, I etched my name proudly in his diary – attesting to my son's efforts.

Reflecting on this incident, I realized that I do sign off on a lot of other things as well, especially at work – one of the responsibilities I have as a principal in the firm. As a firm signatory, I have the 'privilege' of signing a lot of important documents …… at least they look impressive. What does it mean to lend my signature to business-critical documents? What weight does my signature bear? What are the consequences of not reading in detail every legal word? What value do I put on my signature?

Well, when I moved to India during 2005, and during the first few days in my new role, I remember sinking into a deluge of documents waiting to be signed – from approvals for installing coffee machines, ordering new carpets and even making declarations to the tax department!

Here I was getting my Mont Blanc out with a keen excitement to sign these formal contracts …. Quickly I realized, that for most of these documents, my signature was not really the 'expensive' one. It belonged to the CFO or the legal expert.

What then is an 'expensive signature'? To me, an expensive signature is not about affiliations and authority but more about commitment, and taking charge of and pride in your own piece. It's about ownership.

*Just take a moment to think about this – do you add your personal imprint to say a chapter in a project report, a proposal, etc., encouraging the reader/audience to trace the part of the deck back to you? Simply put, do you brand your work as yours……with your unique **special** signature?*

Recently a colleague narrated an incredible tale about a Life Sciences client, who is in the business of making valves that get implanted in human hearts. Apparently, these valves are handcrafted by clinical experts in their U.S. headquarters. The clinical expert stamps the valve with his own initials, a pretty expensive signature, and then it is ready to be shipped to clients (patients) across the globe. Patients from all over the world travel to Irvine to thank the experts who gave them a new lease of life! Imagine that. Imagine your unique capabilities being traced back to you. Imagine the pride!

Imagine for a minute that the client could trace every part of work back to an individual contributor. What if a client were to call you regarding your unique piece? With your signature on it? Would you do anything differently? Would you not then take more ownership?

Well, my younger one is slowly developing a pride in his signature as well. He likes to sign customer survey forms, customs declarations when we are travelling, and even the 'customer copy' of my credit card slip.

He is still figuring out that the merchant copy is the one with the expensive signature.

Mumbai office, April 2010 – Lunchbreak

8.   *My Recipe for Success*

I like cooking. Italian is my specialty, though I do dabble in other cuisines. However, there's one activity that my sons and I indulge on some Sundays – baking cakes or cookies. They are always excited to read the recipe, assemble and measure the required ingredients. It is critical to be precise; otherwise you'll be baking a disaster. The mess in the kitchen drives my wife mad, but we thoroughly enjoy it. It's a great bonding and learning experience.

Cooking is an art and recipes often are well-kept secrets. It is rumoured that only top two executives of Coca-Cola know the formulation of the drink. Similarly, Kentucky Fried Chicken too keeps its blend of spices a closely guarded secret.

Well, there's one recipe that's not exactly a secret. In fact I get asked about it a lot. It's a little time consuming and probably somewhat unique. That's my recipe for success. Interestingly, no two recipes for success are alike as the ingredients, proportions and method vary. So, today I want to share my recipe for success with you. It may look like a fusion recipe gone awry but each ingredient is time tested. I hope you enjoy it.

Success à la Parag

Preparation Time: 8 years Cooking Time: 15 years Serves: many

<u>For the base:</u>

1 portion of Life

1/2 cup passion diced

2 1/2 cup integrity

A pinch of curiosity

3/4 cup commitment

2 tbsp intelligence

3 cups hard work finely chopped

<u>For the filling:</u>

8 tbsp people skills cubed

1 tbsp sense of humour

5 tbsp communication skills

1 tsp ambition

<u>For the dressing:</u>

4 tbsp confidence

3/4 cup innovative bent of mind finely chopped

1/2 cup interests or hobbies

1 cup secret ingredient (to be revealed later)

A dash of luck

For the garnish:

5-7 humility peeled and chopped

2 tsp intuition grated

Directions

Step 1: *In a large bowl, combine passion, integrity, curiosity, commitment, intelligence and hard work with Life. Roll up your sleeves and start working on the mixture with your hands. Yes, it will be hard and maybe even sticky. However, keep kneading till it becomes consistent mixture. Cover the bowl and set it aside for at least five years.*

Result: *You have just made ability to work hard, to manage failures, to constantly question and learn, to steadfast pursue your goals, to love your work and to adhere to a moral and ethical code an intrinsic part of your Life. This is the foundation for success.*

Step 2: *Peel off the cover. Your dough would have doubled in size. Make a fist and punch the dough, till it deflates. After all, you need to figure out how much is only air! In a separate pan flatten your dough. Add people and communication skills, ambition, as well as the sense of humour and roll the dough into a ball. Keep kneading till its smooth and set it aside for at least three more years.*

Result: *You will care about people and their achievements, have the drive to achieve your goals, be consensus driven, articulate your thoughts, laugh at your mistakes and control your ego and also share some of your experiences with others at Step 1. Now, success is just a step away.*

Step 3: *Pre-heat the oven to 225 degrees. Take a large baking dish. Grease it with secret ingredient and place your* *dough in it. Brush it with luck and confidence and arrange hobbies and innovative bend of mind around it. Start baking. Though the warm smell of success will begin to fill the room within minutes, keep baking it for at least 10 years. Keep turning the dough at regular intervals to ensure even baking.*

Result: *The right amount of confidence will find you surrounded by talented and positive people, who will always keep you motivated and energized. According to me, hobbies are essential for they add that extra flavour/zing to Life. Luck will help you be the right person in the right place at the right time. This combination along with constant assessment can eliminate any disaster.*

Once your timer beeps, remove the dish from the oven to cool. Garnish it with humility and grated intuition. Your success is ready to be served. Now, call your family and friends. **Remember success tastes sweeter when you share it with people you love and care. You should be able to enjoy it for years to come.**

PS: *My secret ingredient is adaptability. I've moved through many continents/cities in the last decade. I've moved through many levels (some twice) in the same time. I strongly believe with adaptability, success is always a heartbeat away, no matter how your life unfolds!*

PART 3

The New India Manager

The art of the sailor is to leave nothing to chance

3.1 Breaking Through to 'Managerhood'

The concept of teams has also evolved in the Perfect Storm moment. The term 'team', till the 80s I think, was only used with respect to sports teams. In most workplaces, the vertical structures and the command and control hierarchies meant that each worker had his/her cookie cutter role. Your role would typically not evolve or change until your manager moved on or someone up top retired. Also, your work ethic, motivation, etc. did not really contribute to a manager's evaluation. Compensation increments were a standard affair and rarely linked to actual performance. Though getting to a Manager title was half Olympics.

A friend of my father got a promotion, after twenty years, to manager. He wrote a postcard to my dad with details of how he made it. The title clearly meant a lot to him and those around him. But when he was in his 20s, I can't imagine that his life's plans were around getting there.. What a change from today I thought, where *Gen Yers* want and are expecting a new promotion every year. Manager-hood is just a milestone they quickly want to conquer and be done with.

In those days, a 'manager' was more commonly known as supervisor though. He was essentially one who managed 'labour' or the 'doers'. Today, managers are expected to be doers as well. Big difference. They are accountable for the outputs of not just the 'labour' that sit around their desks but increasingly for managing and coordinating the output of virtual teams, working around the globe. Performance is evaluated based on team work and the manager's performance appraisal is dependent is tied to the success of the project team. Once a project is completed, new teams are formed. New relationships need to be forged. Learnings need to be shared and inclusive environments need to be created. Managers need to make sure that 'players' work well together, help each other and provide back-up support when required. To add to the complexity, not every team will be composed of your star players. Managers need to get the best out of their teams, work their strengths and support tricky areas (*a.k.a* development needs). Hence, a promotion to becoming a manager can be tricky as juniors have choices and managers need to develop people who are motivated to work for them. This notion of choice is a new feature in the perfect storm and today's *Gen Yers* are more than happy to make them.

Over the past decade, the Indian economy has transitioned dramatically from a command and control structure to a market driven environment. The needs of managers have also changed significantly from what they were required to do back then. In the 70s and 80s there was less need of management as we understand 'management' today. In the private sector, the requirement was more to operate through a complex set of typically 'non-value added' rules, handle recalcitrant labour unions affiliated to political parties and execute instructions as handed down through the hierarchy of the organization. This often meant that the manager was not part of the decision making process, his/her only responsibility was to execute and operationalize whatever they were asked to do. Siloed focus was encouraged. The people working under the manager also did not have much of a choice and certainly had no say in the performance review of the manager.

The motivators and subsequent stress levels were very different and the support network at home, typically an extended family environment, was relatively stable. Visiting India back then, I remember uncles, aunts and cousins going off to work and coming home in a fairly routine fashion. Hours were regular, no calls from home, and very little in terms of spillover of work in any form on the home front. The flip-side was that employees were essentially employees for life. It was interesting to me how life was so routine and predictable.

Control on production, lack of import impunity, the noose and labyrinth of regulatory approvals took away every ounce of motivation that a manager or an entrepreneur could harbour. As a result, meritocracy was somewhere stifled between the red tape and the black box of bureaucracy. There was limited contact with the outside world. Communications tools like email were not available and telecommunications services were very expensive. All this in some ways centralized decision making.

Managing global teams was unheard of. For those few who needed to be connected with the outside world it was terribly complicated. I have heard of senior managers during that era for whom a trip abroad meant sleepless nights – getting a visa and foreign exchange was close to Everest climbing sans oxygen tank. These days, 24 hour clocks, conference calls early mornings and late nights are routine. Smartphones make offices incredibly mobile and allow work to spillover to non-office hours.

Another important socio-political trend during this time was that behaving globally was shunned, actually considered unpatriotic. The remnants of nationalism showed up during interactions with India colleagues during the 80s. Brand India was about a few and much eulogized public sectors, nationalized products on the shelf, Doordarshan... For many, staying back in India and getting 'a steady' job was considered a well regarded aspiration ... . Unless you were at the top of the pack, few ventured out of India.

Recently my father called me up from Canada to tell me a year ago about a distant family friend who had died tragically. I had heard about this person, but did not know the full story until I probed my dad that day. He recalled how this young chap had landed at our doorstep back in the 70s. He was barely 20 years old. He had literally run away from home, figured out how to get a visa through some 'middleman' and ended up looking up my dad's name through some distant connection. He came with $20 in his pocket in search of a better life. Through several odd jobs here and there, he survived. Would he have done better staying back in India? Maybe, maybe not.

Landing in Mumbai in 2005 and the few business trips before that were therefore a complete eye-opener for me. The India of the 70s and 80s was vanishing quickly, at least that's how it appeared. Everywhere around me was the glitz of shopping arcades and high rises with English names (Mahogany Towers, Hill View….), even if it meant crossing a few pot holes to get there, youngsters walked confidently talking and texting on their latest mobiles. In fact, it was only after I came to India was I advised by one of my juniors to start a Facebook account. Clearly, connecting was crucial for this New India. It was those changing needs for India's 'New Manager' that motivated me to start connecting more with this group of *Gen Yers*. It was after all this group that would grow into the future 'New India Managers'.

For the first time in the country's modern economic history the demand and opportunities for New India Managers have grown more than the supply. Many Indian companies are looking to become global players and foreign ones who have made significant investments in India are seeking to put into their kitty the 'New India Managers'. I have seen many companies do employee surveys and time and again, the Achilles heel points to 'managerial effectiveness'. This imbalance is driving companies to invest in training and up skilling their managers to handle more complex roles. The New Indian Managers on their part are displaying the fire to learn and upscale skills in order to stake a claim to higher level roles.

The educational background of managers are no more barriers to assimilation of these skills. There is a trend of people building competencies and expertise in roles that do not necessarily supplement their educational background as companies move away from the standard 'engineering and MBA' combo to a more holistic package.

The shift in mindset was changing dramatically especially in the professional services environment in which I was working. All of a sudden, I would be explaining what concepts like meritocracy meant, i.e. that age was no barrier to growth, what matrixed organization structures were and the notion of not really having a boss or many of them. People needed to work in teams, organize around a project manager, get educated about being global and develop a much broader mind-set. In return, however, the expectations from management are also changing. More commitment, tighter deadlines, quality delivery every time were some of the ground rules – no more just clearing files from the 'In' tray to 'Out'. When some of my managers asked project teams to see if they could work through the Diwali holidays to meet a project deadlines, many relished the new opportunities to shine and put in that extra. Though they did ask, 'What's in it for me?' But this request should not be a surprise. In today's world, there are expectations and demands coming from junior employees. They are not shying away from asking for what they want in return for putting in that extra. They now know that age and tenure are no barriers. The *Gen Yers* are relishing this new environment.

So what does it take now to become a 'New India Manager'? From the part of the journey that I have covered and survived, here are some quick notes:

- **Has Global Outlook:** Indian companies today are increasingly looking for best in class ideas and expect to be benchmarked against global best practices. Similarly, when looking for talent again the hunt is global. Indian companies are increasingly taking pride in their multicultural workforce where they hire from world class universities and place them in India. India is also becoming a destination for graduates from leading campuses. It is interesting to note that some of the graduates at leading western universities are willing to relocate to India at a salary much less that what they possibly could earn abroad just to get the 'India experience' on their CVs. Consequently, managers in India are getting a chance to work with 'western' colleagues not only when the leave India's borders but also within India itself. The global outlook is manifested in two critical areas: an ability to work across cultures and time-zones. In this context culture is not just western but also includes, Japanese, Chinese, Koreans, Middle East and even African and an ability to work with virtual teams located across the world. While learning a new language like Spanish, German or even Chinese is an option, New India Managers need to invest time in upgrading their core English business communications skills. Succinctly communicating with virtual teams has becoming incredibly important to drive virtual team efficiency and effectiveness.

- **Seeks empowerment** – Today's New India Managers are seeking out opportunities to make decisions and opportunities to demonstrate situational leadership.

They are not necessarily waiting for a promotion or a title to command respect. While *Gen Yers* are pushing for change, it is still taking time for empowerment to work its way down the hierarchy in many organizations but change is happening. I have seen it happening in highly successful services companies where even a waiter can 'make a call' on customizing a menu item for restaurant patron. Or a call centre operator going out of his/her way to 'break policy' in order to satisfy a customer request. There will be times when they take 'empowerment' a bit too far and get rapped on their knuckles, but this generation is not worried about that outcome. They are looking to push the boundaries.

• **Collaborates across hierarchies, works laterally across diverse teams** – The Indian manager is making a transition from an individual performance based management systems to performance systems which reward and recognize ability to team with colleagues in many cases from across the globe. In addition, countless studies have supported the idea that companies are looking for increasingly diverse working teams to drive superior performance and new ideas. So not only is teaming becoming essential, teaming across cultures, genders, demographics, etc. is becoming increasingly important. Hierarchal management structures are also giving way to collaboration across organizations and is becoming independent of nationality and time zones. The need for collaboration is being by a push to increase efficiency and faster development cycles, many times working the 24-hr 'follow the sun' approach and frankly to drive new product innovation as new ideas are emerging throughout global organizations.

- **Expects to be rewarded for outcomes vs inputs** – New India Managers are willing to take risks and work globally across diverse teams, but they are also looking to be measured differently. It is no longer about the number of hours worked or even booking 'overtime' (a concept that seems to have disappeared), it's all about output and productivity. What value has been generated for the company, not how many hours were worked. Performance management systems are catching up but still have way to go. They are also getting more comfortable that their individual performance is tied to the success of the project team and/or the organization. These managers are tracking company performance (many are partially compensated by stock options and shares) and are personally invested in companies ... a big change from 20-30 years ago.

- **Motivator and mentor** – New India Managers are expected to provide mentorship to junior colleagues are a much earlier age in their careers. Their 10 years of experience over the past decade is much more relevant for junior colleagues than the 30+ years of experience of the previous generation. This group knows that the mentoring of junior colleagues is core to their own personal success as well.

The challenge with these attributes is that there were no courses in university that taught these attributes. The vast majority of schools and colleges are not preparing students to become future managers as in many cases individual performance is main focus and hierarchy is the rule. Companies are having to invest heavily in driving this transition.

For a few current managers, hitting the storm and the transition to the New India Manager has been a wake-up call. Seniority and longevity no longer matter. Their titles which commanded respect only a few years ago are ignored. In a country like India with its deep rooted culture and faith in respecting elders, one can imagine the conflicting thoughts and ideas whirling around in their minds. With the *Gen Yers* approaching rapidly behind them, they need to be able to shift into a different gear. A few have made the pivot, adapted and navigated to become a true leader, taking some risks that could have scared off the faint of heart. I applaud this group who are now in a position to give back to the *Gen Yers*.

Unfortunately there have been some casualties along the way. In most circumstances, these professionals were not able to 'adjust their sails' and work through different and more complex storms. They relied on what had worked in the past but this storm is different. Not able to adapt and read the wind, they were forced to change course and unfortunately many will continue to be caught up in the storm for years to come until they figure out the new rules of the game. For this group, they rested on their title – 'Manager'. Was that not supposed to command respect? Why did the juniors not want to work for them, let alone go that extra mile? Where did they fall short in terms of being able to motivate this new generation?

I met a few of these professionals. They were top performers only a few years earlier in an era that quickly changed on them. In my role, I had to have the conversations with them explaining how their future in our organization at least was not very certain. I would repeat the line that 'people leave people, people do not leave organizations'. The conversations were difficult, for them obviously, but for me also. I recall saying to myself that I didn't sign up for this ... or did I? Perhaps these discussions were new learnings for me as well.

Breaking through to becoming the new India Manager is a tricky task that seems to be top of mind for many new professionals in India. The 'Manager' title carries a lot of weight and is an important milestone to share with family and friends. The timelines to getting to this important career milestone has though changed considerably as in the 70s and 80s, people worked for years before achieving this title.

3.2 Women at the Helm

She must find a boat and sail in it. No guarantee of shore. Only a conviction that what she wanted could exist, if she dared find it.

For women in India there is an added layer with life events and an even more complex social infrastructure. They face a critical choice of whether to continue working or staying at home post marriage or child birth – their decision of course is taken on that 'sacrifice' table. The traditional family structure effects even urban, educated women, and many in our office are the first in their families to step outside and have a career. They are constantly pulled from all sides to conform to the image of ideal wife, ideal daughter and ideal daughter-in-law. I routinely hear about so many women, exceptional professionals and managers at work, who get up at 4am, make elaborate breakfasts, pack lunchboxes for family and often extended family, put in a full day of hard work, go back (some directly enter the kitchen) make dinner, clean up, check home work .... at the same time managing different emotions and grouses that the in-laws have packed in the day!

The topic of developing and retaining women in the workforce has emerged as a critical issue for corporates in India because if India is to maintain its pace, it will need to tap this mine of educated and talented resources much more than it has in the past. Nearly 50% of the population cannot be ignored and countless business cases on the topic all lead to the same conclusion. No rocket-science here.

The key issue though is asking what causes women to leave the workforce? Are these the same challenges as in the West? How is this generation different from the earlier one? At first sight, from an outsider's perspective, women in India have more cushions. They typically do not have to deal with a lot of travel and it would appear that they have the 'home infrastructure', a.k.a in-laws and maids, in place.

We regularly have senior women professionals visit our offices from overseas. A typical agenda topic is for them to sit down with other women managers and discuss challenges and potential solutions for our women professionals in India. In one instance, one of the visitors came up to me after the session and was astonished that women in India (at a Manager level at least) had drivers, did not have to travel out of town as much, had a cook and even parental and in-law support to take care of children. Wow, she said, if only we had that social infrastructure in the west! She recalled how many phone calls she needed to make regularly with her Bluetooth on while folding laundry ...balancing the remote management of her kids as she travelled for 4-5 days a week.

I did remind her that she had not seen the flip side which included that 4 am to midnight ritual that women had to go through in India. In India, especially for women, it's all about keeping several things in the air at one time … kids, maids, work, husbands, in-laws… But what happens when one of those items drop? Well it really depends now doesn't it? Are you juggling eggs or oranges?

I have had several manager-level women professionals come to me to discuss their careers and options for the future. I realize that our profession is very challenging and frankly, we have thrown every flexibility policy possible to help address the issue of retaining high potential women in the firm. Unfortunately, we still lose the battle many a time. One such senior manager came to me with her challenge. She said that, 'it was not worth it'. 'The sacrifices that I am making, and still I get no recognition'. (By the way, I realized that simply because she had even come to me asking for support was a big step from the 70s and 80s when women, whatever their numbers were in the corporate workplace, were maybe conditioned to take it all on themselves and never speak up.)

I continued the dialogue to better understand the 'recognition' aspect and she was disappointed at a missed promotion. Eventually she left the firm. My guess is it really was not the promotion but rather the 'recognition', both at work and in her personal space that she aspired for. Then there was another woman manager who did not wait for token appreciations but had a clear personal plan in place. I found her self-advocacy very refreshing.

In India's changing professional landscape, we also have great women role models who have emerged in the past decade, primarily in the financial services and consumer business sectors. Women have also been graduating in pretty decent numbers from MBA schools and other universities. But what happened to all of those who graduated in the mid 90's? Though perhaps relatively few in number, they would have been the ideal role models that this new generation needs so desperately. And we would have done better than the 5-6 % of women representation in corporate boards.

At a dinner, I met one such woman, who told me that only a small fraction of those women who were in her MBA class were actually working today! What a shame I thought ... again members of the 'tip of the iceberg' not really having the passion and/or mentorship to continue to navigate the storm to provide the much needed leadership India so desperately needs. On the positive side, I have met a few of these women who have moved away from the corporate pace to work for NGOs and/or have set up their own ventures. My take-away is that women in leadership roles today need to be part of the solution. While they clearly have been the pioneers, they need to connect with the new generation of women and make their road easier ... not more difficult.

At one of the regular conferences, a woman leader on the podium went on to describe her situation in which a junior female practitioner wanted some extra time off after returning from maternity leave in the middle of a critical project. She described how she was in two minds as she re-called her own career path in which she 'did not get any breaks' to get to where she was today. At the same time, she wanted to demonstrate that as a woman she could empathize with the lady's situation. These dilemmas go through senior women professionals' minds all of the time. In today's India, the choices should be easy, we need to flood our organizations with women and do what we can to ensure that they are able to make it. Thinking back to my life, my dad made it easier for me not in terms of spoiling me, but in terms of giving me a higher platform than what he had. In today's India, given the steep slope of the growth curve, we need to give an even higher platform for those behind us.

This set of blogs talks about getting to the next level beyond managerhood. At this stage you start to set your eyes on success at the next level and get a peek into leadership. It takes new techniques and strategies to get you there. Opportunities will be few, but you need to grasp them even if it takes you off the beaten path and out of your comfort zone. Just to make it more complicated, others are trying to navigate to the same destination as the pinnacle of any organization can only accommodate a selected few.

Mumbai, May 2010 – Early Sunday morning

1.   Taking off the Blinders

In life, we sometimes turn into racehorses.

One of the unique experiences in India has been going to the races. I have been a few times in Mumbai and once in Kolkata. While not quite Ascot, it is a pretty formal affair. Given that I was not experienced in the horses and gambling thing, a friend took me down to the see the horses prior to them being walked on the track.

Seeing them up close and personal revealed how limiting the horses' blinkers were. They literally have no peripheral vision. This severely limits their vision, forces them to focus on the track ahead and be unperturbed by other horses or the loud cheering. After all, the race is about winning.

Likewise, we don our blinkers to touch a finish line and when we don't need distractions. We zero in on our goals because winning is crucial to us. While this focus is important for short 'sprints' and achieving milestones at the workplace, we need not be horses, always. The workplace is not a Derby after all. There is more to life than staying in your lane. In fact, leadership demands getting out of this comfort zone and taking off your blinkers.

With our blinkers on, we clearly see the straight road ahead, but have no peripheral vision. This means losing sight of the larger picture. Over time, it promotes complacency, creates a false sense of security, and limits possibilities. Yet, we continue with our blinkered approach – for it is comfortable and safe - our 'happy' places. Research proves highly successful people, especially leaders, view life more broadly and have a wider perspective. Also in many ways, they appreciate revisiting their 'comfort zones' a lot more. A colleague from the US moved to India and was clearly out of his 'comfort zone'. For some months he and his wife didn't quite unpack their suitcases. Very slowly they adjusted to the chaos and the charm around them. When it was time for them to repatriate back, they had a clear list of 'Things I will miss most about Mumbai…"

I strongly believe like any other habits, the habit of wearing blinkers can also be broken. It only calls for a sense of adventure, courage, risk-taking and ironically some focus.

Here are a few examples for making a beginning:

Explore a new place: *I have relocated from Canada to Hong Kong to China to India, in a matter of 10 years. It did require adapting to new cultures, cities, work-styles, people, as well as climates. While it was not easy at the time, looking back, I wouldn't change a thing. Explore newer worlds* *when given the chance and experience the difference. The challenges of settling in will quickly fade away.*

Start something new: *I tried new things. I have jumped out of a plane (with a parachute, of course!), sampled East Asian 'delicacies' (some were still moving in my plate), and started blogging. The idea is to be adventurous; to broaden your horizons. Learn a new language, take lessons in dancing or art, read an unfamiliar author/genre, the options are infinite.*

One step beyond: *I have often needed to network with a very different set of leaders, many of whom I have only admired from a distance. It was at first uncomfortable and intimidating, but you learn to fit in. You listen and participate. This happened in the first executive meeting that I attended back in the US. Awkwardly, I took a seat at one of the side tables, away from the core group sitting around the 'U-shaped' conference seating arrangement. I kind of felt more comfortable being slightly away from the crowd. After the break, I nudged into the 'inner circle'. It gave me new perspectives – some that I had not known even after several years with the organization. So, move beyond your circle. You never know what doors it might open for you.*

Return to innocence: *Finally, don't forget the power of returning to your comfort zone. Mine is watching a great Michael Douglas movie or playing an early morning round of golf. It wipes out the stress of the previous week and allows me to re-charge. I revisit my zone, regularly. So, should you.*

So, how do you stop being a racehorse? The answer is to take off your blinkers once in a while and step out.

British Airways Flight, October 2012 – Flying back London to Mumbai

2. The Global Nomad

This month I was in **the** United States (for those who have seen *English Vinglish*). As expected, most of the networking buzz was around the Romney-Obama debates. Though I was able to engage with both camps, at the back of my mind I did feel a bit out of place. Something like when I was watching a recent Twenty20 cricket final between the West Indies and Sri Lanka … keen how the game unfolds…. but my heart was really not into it without India in the finals.

During one such conversation, it occurred to me that the last time I had actually voted (other than for those internal officer polls) was over 20 years ago, in Canada. You see, my situation is a bit one-off. I am a Canadian citizen, hold a leadership position with a U.S firm, Indian resident (pay my taxes here), and a Hong Kong permanent resident. Given my movements over the past 20 + years, and the relative (lack of) drama in Canadian politics, I was frankly never motivated to exercise my voting rights.

After the meeting, I reached Toronto over the weekend, to visit my parents, my brother, and his family. During a lazy chit-chat with my nephew, I was curious to find out about if at all he was inspired by his "global one-off" uncle. He quickly came back to me, "I am never moving out of Canada". More existential thoughts followed after this abrupt dismissal by kin! So, am I really what business jargon tags as - 'a professional nomad'? Maybe, I guess.

I do believe that in today's globally connected economies, whether you end up being a professional nomad or want to establish your roots in a country of choice, you need to develop 'global fluency'. Simply put, it means you need to feel like a citizen of the world, in addition to the country which you call 'home'. 'Going Global' is no more just an option and right now at there is really a great need for professionals who think like global citizens. It begins with simple things:

Be 'connected' – Take an interest about elections in other countries, global businesses that could disrupt industries, trends in the global talent landscape, and such

Acquire a passion for diversity – Appreciate cultural nuances, capitalize on differences, be comfortable in uncomfortable environments

Build trusting virtual relationships – It starts with empathy and respect for the other, by observing and listening more

Finally, when I get back 'home' (after seven years, I like calling Mumbai 'home'), catching up with my boys …. the younger one asks, "So Dad, who is going to win the US elections?" Few months ago, this young Obama fan wrote a neat one-pager to the American President.

"A close race likely," I answer in all seriousness that the conversation deserves. … "but Obama should pull through…" I play Dad to the T, keeping hope alive in the young heart. "That's too bad, I am hoping for the other guy, because Obama never replied back really!" the nine year old shockingly lets out.

Sounds like one of those undecided voters back in the United States!

On a flight back to Mumbai Feb 2008 – Thinking about the upcoming International Women's Day

3.   Be the breakthrough, not barrier

Imagine if it was a male CEO at Yahoo!, making that cavalier command – 'No more work-from-home!' Media would have whipped up double the frenzy, activists would have had a field day, blogsphere would be spammed with how the corporate world is still an "old boys' network". But here we have a woman, a famous new mother, spinning a gender unfriendly decree, hounded by her own fraternity. For once, there must be a few relieved men around! I have known and worked with women professionals – all talented, ambitious women, beating the pulp out of every gender stereotype. However a moment of truth for me, as I started connecting the dots – 'Women don't seem to understand each other sometimes'. (While I wouldn't really use marginalized experiences as a trend … it did make me sit up and think and ask a few questions.)

Questions ran in my mind (and I added a slice of my own 'neutral' observations):-

- *Have I seen women readily extending help or their network to other women colleagues?*
- *Do up-and-coming women professionals see themselves as pioneers of sorts, especially in markets like India? Are they preparing themselves well enough to dent the Fortune numbers?*
- *Were there women who reached the pinnacle and slammed the door behind them?*

- *Are women bosses more threatened by a high-performing woman than by other male colleagues?*
- *Stereotypical perhaps, but do women subordinates prefer their female bosses to display more 'feminine attributes' like empathy and sensitivity versus decisive and analytical?*

What at times stops women, at all levels, from helping each grow and strengthen their own clan! What happened to that therapeutic women bonding? Sisters-for-life?

I would love to see more back-slapping camaraderie (infamous, but it works)? ; an old girls 'club ("let's play pebble" talk is a great binder)? ; connecting outside office (women can be so much more creative in this case...we men usually land up in the same places)? On a serious note – find a women mentor and confidante, ask each other for counsel and career tips, applaud each other for personal and professional highs, give each other business advice and chances, promote each other more at client meetings and team outings, encourage each other to take risks and challenges…

In short, devise ways to be each other's breakthrough, not barrier. We are all listening.

MIT Campus, Pune – September 2012 – Waiting for the management interview schedule

4.   So, who is this New Manager?

It was during my early Consulting days at Hong Kong that I had to meet a local leader over lunch. I was still coming to terms with the Chinese work style, identifying their personality and performance hot buttons. In public, I called their food '*interesting*', took lessons in Mandarin after work hours, became more easy with their long leisurely business lunches versus the "**looking at the watch kinds**". When the senior leader took the liberty of ordering an octopus dish, I went with him. I had to tell myself that such an opportunity may not come up again!

On our plates were served wriggling pieces of colourless molluscs .... There was no looking back, we spoke about business as I chewed on .... live 'gummi bear' inside my mouth. By that evening some great relationships were built, and the price of swallowing live sea creatures seemed little.

What it taught me was the ability to experiment outside my comfort zone.

It was the early nineties, Asia was booming, my focus was in the area of telecommunications and every market was de-regulating turning monopolies into fully competitive environments. We had a relatively small group of 40-50 consultants in Hong Kong who were extremely busy – and we were also having a lot of fun! Each time we went back to Canada for a vacation, it seemed that very few things were changing back home. Between Hong Kong and Canada I *had built a global bridge of sorts….balancing cultures and distances. I had started feeling like a global citizen, more so when my kids were born at a Hong Kong government hospital. The world was not only shrinking but was folding over, more neatly than we imagine, and into our pockets.*

This was also the passage of time for the New Manager in India. A breed that was storming the flat corporate world, looking for very different goals than the earlier generations and was impatient with bureaucracy, wanted quick results, sought empowerment, was more at home with happenings around the globe. To my mind the New India Manager would stand out in a crowd on account of the following traits:

Collaborates; *transcending hierarchies, domains and geographies. To the New Manager, teaming across cultures, time zones, domains, or hierarchies is all in a day's work.*

Sees *the larger context, the wider perspective. They look at the entire jigsaw, not individual pieces. They push for a broader perspective to deliver the best results.*

Adapts *and* ***innovates.*** *Deals with change, often rapid and radical. They proactively redefine and improve themselves to better align with a changing organization and environment.*

Influences, articulates, persuades. *For the team, the New Manager navigates through ambiguity, mitigates risks, encourages open communications, manages stakeholders' expectations, and drives a team to deliver results.*

Motivates *and* ***coaches.*** *Creates leaders not followers. Hierarchy breeds dependence. The New Manager invests time in their team, as they believe that leadership belongs* to everyone. *Their legacy will be defined by the number of leaders they create not the number of people they manage.*

*Drives towards a **vision** not a goal - The New Manager envisions the destination and establishes a roadmap with timelines to get there.*

*The New Manager has tough work hours, yet maintains a **career-life fit.** I met one the other day on a trip to one of our offices. He used to work in India, shifted to the US for five years and decided to move back. I asked whether he had moved back because of family reasons and he said not really. He explained how he felt that after five years he had got a great learning experience but felt that he could leverage this experience more effectively out of India. He could contribute to the management team, start mentoring others and deliver the same client experience from India.* **Now there's a New India Manager!**

Los Angeles, August 2009 – Finishing a round of presentations for Partner admission

5. *The Curious Case of Manav Anand*

Manav Anand (name changed) is in his early thirties. He loves his job, keeps expected (long) hours and defines a dedicated and hardworking professional. He is comfortable with his peers and managers. If the corporate world were a mountain, Manav has ambitions to keep climbing and eventually reach the summit.

Yet, he has been in his present role for over five years. This year too, he isn't with the group ascending to the next point. He is still at Camp II, a bit frustrated and perhaps even dejected. He feels that luck is not on his side.

We have several Manavs (across all levels). They believe mountaineering is just about a steady climb – keep climbing and one eventually gets there. That's the fallacy. It is much bigger and broader. It is about strategizing and planning; teamwork and leadership; mitigating challenges; taking bold and deliberate risks; having the right equipment; learning from failures; fitness levels; knowledge and experience and the climb. Don't forget that challenges or the terrain will change at different stages of the climb. Also, the higher you climb, the narrower the route and thinner the oxygen. Therefore, only a determined few actually make it to the top.

But, Manav can take heart, as all is not lost. The important thing is to identify and learn from missed opportunities. Let's examine some of these missed chances and ideas to avoid them:

Limited by his job title: *Manav met expectations. However, to move to the next level, he needs to think, act, and perform at that next level.*

Idea: *Remember, you are just not an employee, but the architect of your career. You have to think beyond your level and make constant attempts to grow your career. Grab internal opportunities such as new projects and initiatives to enrich your experience.*

No action plan: *Manav has some vague high-level goals, but no action plan to achieve them. Just wanting something is not enough to make it happen.*

Idea: *The best way to achieve any goal is by making an action plan for it. If Manav's long-term goal was to climb the summit, then he needed several short-term goals to help him get there. Be S.M.A.R.T. about your goals. Even then, at times, the best of plans fail. No matter, tweak your plan and get back on track.*

Not investing in his capabilities: *In a world of constant change, Manav needed to be flexible and on top of things. But he never invested in himself. He wanted a long-term career in an area of expertise, which is no longer the flavour of the season.*

Idea: *Business continues to evolve. So must we. What was 'in' yesterday is 'out' tomorrow. Failing to adjust can result in missed opportunities. Become instrumental and mission critical, again! Remember how you immersed yourself and became the 'go to person' on the floor back at base camp? Re-live that experience.*

Not taking a break: *Our careers form an important part of our lives, but other areas need our attention too. Manav was too work focussed and was almost nearing a burnout. His momentum was not enough to get him past the goal line.*

Idea: *We need to rest and recharge to deliver optimal performance. Working unreasonably long hours, for extended periods can wear us out and deprive us of the ability to provide fresh and creative ideas. Ideas are the fuel on which the career engine runs. Learn how to stop being a racehorse.* **So, let's revisit lost opportunities, clear out the cobwebs, re-energize, rejuvenate, and ready ourselves for the climb. They say the view is always better from the top.**

New York, February 17, 2012 – Wall Street …
Another round of Partner presentations

6.   Breaking Through the Clouds

This is Wall Street, the heart of Corporate America. As I look around, it is difficult not to be impressed, notwithstanding the current economic slump, the Occupy Wall Street slogans, and the Euro zone financial crisis.

Earlier this morning, as I walk from my hotel to office, I find myself stop and read the inlaid brass plates, mounted along the sidewalk. These plates, document key events (I am told 'ticker tape parades'), in honour of famous people, who made historic visits to Wall Street over the years. I am especially proud to see a nameplate that reads "Jawaharlal Nehru, October 17, 1949."

I read the plates carefully, one by one. And there was a familiar pattern! Each of them bears the name of a man – Albert Einstein, Theodore Roosevelt, Charles Lindbergh, Dwight Eisenhower, Bobby Jones…

Think about it. Corporate America, at the end of the day, was created by men – Ford, Rockefeller, Welch, Buffett, Bloomberg, and so on. This is a fact that few can argue with.

*So, I am excited when I come to a brass plate that reads – **"June 20, 1932 – Amelia Earhart Putnam following transatlantic flight."** Wow! I remember the story of this 'noted American aviation pioneer and author', her transatlantic flight, and her sensational disappearance over the Pacific Ocean a few years later in 1937.*

So, here in the heart of Corporate America, a male bastion, a female 'pioneer' had managed to leave a mark!

Standing in front of this particular inscription, I am reminded of our women professionals back home …

This is also my chance to reach out to our women professionals and share with them my homegrown 'Lessons from Amelia'.

Be the trendsetter not the hanger-on *– Amelia accepted the fact that she was a pioneer. It is interesting that from an early age she maintained a scrapbook of newspaper clippings about successful women in predominantly 'male-oriented' fields. She adapted herself to 'play in a field' that was not originally cut out for women. There is a story that she cut her hair and started to wear a leather jacket to join the male pilot club.*

Lead from the Front *– While I am sure that she could have benefited from other women mentors (very few around that time), she knew that she would need to become one of those future mentors. She paved the way and made it easier for a future generation of women pilots. She also started an organization devoted to female flyers. She wanted to make the path easier for the next generation… certainly did not feel that* **"women were women's worst enemies."**

Swing back out of the cloudbank *– Amelia understood early on that she would need to work harder to achieve her goals. In her case, while she was competent and intelligent, she was not the "best pilot or naturally gifted to become a pilot." She had several potential mishaps including one serious miscalculation, where she came spinning down through a cloudbank, only to reemerge at 3,000 ft.*

Seek help when you need it – *Amelia acknowledged her limitations as a pilot and often sought assistance throughout her career from various instructors versus trying to go solo.*

Strike that balance… you know how to do it best – *Amelia balanced her ambition with a need/desire to look after her parents. She spent considerable time with her recently divorced mother. In her marriage, she believed herself to be an 'equal breadwinner'.*

Your challenges are real – *Amelia represents 'real' challenges (she could ill afford higher studies due to lack of funds, she had health issues, and her parents went through separation). This in contrast to many other famous women leaders, who were either born for greatness (think Marie Curie, Judith Polgar) or were handed greatness in legacy (think Queen Elizabeth, Indira Gandhi). She represents a more realistic role model for women.*

The good news is that in India we are fast growing our own Amelias (4 Indians amongst Fortune's Top 50 women leaders as of Oct 2013). India Parliament needs to take some lessons here …. those who are breaking through the clouds… those who do not seek other women to lead them but are comfortable to be at the forefront… those who realize that they are blazing the trail versus following a beaten path… those who are paving the way for the future generation of women leaders.

While all those great men, embossed on the Wall Street plaques, shone in the cool New York morning sunlight, ***I thought how the recent economic crisis would have been very different if the infamous bank was called 'Lehman Sisters' instead!***

7.   *Blue Collar Leader*

Do you recall a T.V commercial for an iconic Indian watch brand ? It had Bollywood superstar Aamir Khan playing a character who makes a house call to fix a computer. The twist is at end of this 40-second commercial – it is revealed that the character whom everyone assumed to be a shop assistant, was the head-honcho of the organization, much to the shock and awe of the customer. Despite his title and visible perks (uniformed chauffer and Mercedes Benz), the character had no qualms rolling up his sleeve and attending to a mere service call. For him, it was all in a day's work. He epitomized a new breed of corporate leaders – the blue collared.

Before I explain further – here's a list of the first paycheques of some top C-suite leaders today:

- *Steve Jobs, who needs no introduction started as a technician for videogame maker Atari*
- *Larry Ellison, Oracle CEO started as a programmer*
- *Barry Salzberg, Deloitte CEO, started as a payroll clerk for the New York Board of Education*
- *Michael Dell washed dishes at a local Chinese restaurant*
- *Lenovo founder Liu Chuanzhi started as a rice farmer*

*Read the list carefully. Every name on that list had a modest beginning. They've working class backgrounds, yet went on to occupy the top echelons in the corporate world. They define blue collar leaders. They combined their talent, passion and knowledge with commitment, perseverance and hard work to become the best in their field. Consequently, the nameplate in the corner office is rightfully theirs. **To them, success or leadership is never a prerogative, it was always earned.***

So, how do you recognize a blue collar leader?

- *They are not demi-gods confined to their corner offices. Instead, they have an affinity for others; they're affable and they like people. Most often, this breed is seen walking the halls chatting with people.*

- *They strongly believe that leadership is about creating leaders and not followers. Mentoring or coaching comes naturally to them.*

- *They are your modern-day master craftsmen. In ancient Europe, artisans had to pass through the career chain from apprentice to journeyman before being celebrated as a master craftsmen. It was a long and hard journey, where the artisan had to prove their abilities and passion for the craft at every juncture. There were no shortcuts. Likewise, our blue collar leaders have spent a lifetime mastering the art. They have a deep understanding of the business. You cannot fake knowledge or experience.*

- *They are not constantly comparing their relative success (though they can be extremely competitive) with others, but more focused on achieving absolute success.*

- *They are distinctly humble, yet proud and confident of their success. They never forget their roots. That's critical to their success. So, they have no qualms in rolling up their sleeves and getting their hands dirty every now then. Aamir's character probably started his multi-million dollar corporation fixing computers in his bedroom. Hence, he didn't think twice before making a service visit.*

Well, I must confess, I've borrowed this term from a senior Partner in our firm. He mentioned it on his visit to India. It didn't quite hit me till I saw the commercial. Interesting how some dots get connected in life. Incidentally, he too should be in the list above!

PART 4

Leadership and Next

4.1 Leaders Ahoy!

I have had the opportunity to work with several exceptional leaders in my career both from within the organization and some outside of it. A couple of leaders however really stand out in my memory. Both from within the firm (not unnatural when you start at a place at 22 and decide to stick on for the next 25 years. Obviously, you have met some exceptional people indoors and have not needed to look out that much). While not perfect by any stretch (an interesting finding in itself – leaders are not perfect), both have influenced my leadership style immensely. The common trait was a focus on high performance and an ability to connect/ show empathy with both teams and clients.

One was my first office managing director in Ottawa who stood out for his imposing personality, personal aura, attention to detail and his ability to connect with people. He stood tall figuratively and in reality at 6 feet 4 inches. I would call him one of the founding fathers of the management consulting field, and he was frequently quoted as such. I recall walking past his office and he would have these file folders neatly sorted on the floor of his office for each of his clients - colour coded with *to dos* listed against each one. He really introduced me to this relatively new profession of management consulting which helped businesses solve their most complex problems. I also learned how to write or more importantly, the importance of being able to write in a structured manner.

On the personal side, I cannot imagine that a leader in any organization would go out of his way to invite new campus grads to their home and even cook them a meal! A few of us new grads were fortunate to watch him put together a dinner – done with the precision of a watch maker. We were also able to connect a few times on the squash court though with his imposing frame and left handed shots, it was not much fun for most of us.

But it was his ability to connect with people that was different. In our first week in the office, he came to meet the new campus recruits, I was one of two, and said in a bold and boisterous voice, *"Welcome and look forward to you becoming a Partner in ten years!"* 'Partner in ten years!' not considered a long time in those days, resonated and this statement alone clearly defined my path forward.

His level of preparedness was exceptional. For example, in those days plugging in a laptop to a projector was not the norm and we used transparencies on overhead projectors. He would make sure to keep an extra projector bulb in his pocket in case the light went out in the middle of his talk.

Another exceptional leader was my office managing director, this time in Hong Kong. He taught us how to think and not hide behind the all too common jargon that we sometimes pick up in our professions. His instruction was – "Don't come to me with a recycled presentation. To our horror, he would tear our decks apart if we loaded our slides with our comforting consulting jargon. His mantra was focus on originality and learn the industry. Once hired by a client, he would say, *"We do not have the right to not understand the subject. We have to learn it."* I remember being in rooms with him when he 'wowed' clients with an unequalled depth of subject matter.

His immaculate dressing style was another leadership intangible. Forcing us to keep pace, we had a tailor visit the office regularly and someone who used to come to shine everyone's shoes. My double pocketed shirt 'imported from Canada' was a quick casualty. I remember him even asking a colleague to leave the office one morning to purchase a belt as this colleague had forgotten to wear his that day. "Every professional needs to represent our brand", he would say. A professional has to deliver the entire package.

Coming to India, I had the opportunity to leverage some of these learnings. Leadership in India has always been a big deal. While political leaders have scaled down over the years in the trust and imagination of the common people, hero worshipping film stars and cricketers has taken on a whole new meaning in this country. During my early encounters with Indian mom and pop stores and auto rickshaws, I would invariably have a film star in shades, or a cricketer with folded arms, smiling at me out of numerous sized posters. Isn't anybody who fuels the imagination and aspiration of the followers a leader?

And then there were leaders in public sectors and the government offices who came with a life time guarantee. In those days, walking on a company floor meant that everyone would stand up from what they were doing and literally salute the leader's presence. The leader was mostly invisible and referred to in third person, his personal assistant wielded power by dropping bits of information about what 'Sir' said or did. In short, hierarchies were vacuum sealed, no one questioned it. I am sometimes reminded of Orwell's *1984 when* I try to imagine how offices functioned in the *Licence Raj* days. There were perhaps undercurrents of fear, awe, speculation, and subservience among the 'led', but it was perhaps counterbalanced by the insular, stress-free nature of roles. You had 10 files to clear by 5 pm and then go home. What did it matter how and what the leader thought? For other challenges, there was the Union at work. In contrast, I think about the number of times professionals, across levels, have blocked my calendar (sometimes impromptu visits) to discuss an unfair rating, a missed onsite assignment etc... the walls just got swallowed.

Indian business executives in the 80s and early 90s were charting totally new waters. To add to the ambiguity, much of their business etiquette and culture (unlike China and Korea) was unabashedly borrowed from the West. Tight suits, choking ties, handshakes, business jargons, getting a grasp of Sensex markets, quick MBAs, and yet retaining leadership values and old habits picked from around and about. These leaders were thus more flexible and risk taking (markets were opening up), more resilient and accommodating (challenges of infrastructure and a regulatory atmosphere continued), they had started to understand that ladders and labels may no longer be effective. A detached and despotic management style gave way to an inclusive and democratic leadership... the captains of the ships now started to rewrite the rules of leadership. Yet the old school loyalty, humility and diligence stayed on – a good mix in all, I'd say.

At such a time, with lessons from my inimitable leaders, tucked under my sleeves, I entered the India workplace, ready to try out a few of them at least. I steered teams through good markets and bear runs on the Sensex, through top '1' ratings and missed promotions, through resource crunches and low business cycles, through happy clients and disgruntled ones, through never before seen floods and bomb threats (something that I had not experienced in Canada or in Hong Kong)... and a few things got embossed on life's footnotes – *'Leaders need to have a high tolerance for risk and failure, have the endurance for ambiguity, sometimes lead on the fly, be disruptive if need be, have the courage to shun conventional thinking and then balance it with practical and reasonable judgments, all the way be super adaptable, hands-on, but finally call the shots. You have to also be comfortable in knowing that you will be building something that will be transitioned sooner or later. You need to work yourself out of your job. Roles do not last forever and neither should they ... unless you are heading a totalitarian regime.'*

Our team in India was growing breakneck and to support the growth we were seriously nurturing a coterie of responsible 'locally hired, home grown' leaders, as opposed to, those who appeared trough an expat route. In 2005, there were few senior leaders, but now, nearly ten years later, there were several who had braved the storm and were establishing their presence in the organization both in India and around the globe. Proudly, there were a couple of women who had also made the pioneering journey. Beyond learning how to navigate the storm, one of the most important parts of their journey was their ability to 'stay ahead' of the swell of the *Gen Yers* coming behind them – a lot that were unlike their peers with whom they grew up.

I have met such 'home grown' leaders who have crossed the chasm to become true global leaders in other organizations in India, the ones that braved the perfect storm. They were able to adapt and shift to the realities of leading in a new India environment. I have also met many in social circles who were drop shipped from overseas, the NRI 'I want to return home' candidates, many of whom frankly complained more than actually trying to even understand how to navigate the storm in this now 'new India' – nothing like the Motherland they left behind several years earlier. Of this lot, there were a few who were able to dive in fully and make it work with solutions not simply lifted and shifted from the west but with ideas that were customized for this new India. They realized quickly that life in India had changed dramatically since they had left. It was not only about obvious infrastructure improvements or that you could get home delivered pizza. This subset of NRIs realized that expectations were changing rapidly especially among the *Gen Yers*. More importantly, their expectations from leadership was evolving. This new generation was not looking for marching orders, solid line reporting relationships, opportunities to address their leaders as 'sir' or like in the 70s and 80s an opportunity to get the one-way ticket to the west. They were looking for leaders who could develop more leaders and not simply followers.

The *Gen Yers*, as they are in a hurry about everything (blame it on internet speed), want to quickly and clearly trudge up the path to leadership. One that is not dependent on nepotism, mindless in between structures, waiting periods, and pure luck. Meritocracy is the new mantra. "If I am ready to lead, why should I not break the line?" By which age did you become a partner – this is one of the favourite questions the *Gen Y* group asks me during my chat session with them. 34, I tell them. And I read their minds – "Well, that was years ago, if I can get it right, I can easily bring it down to below 30." In fact is there not a short-cut? Why even ten years?

And the *Gen Yers* clearly want to learn the ropes early on. And why not? Frankly speaking, we wait too long to grow 'leaders' per se. The eligibility criteria being – you need to see the full cycle of things, grow a few grey hair in your sideburns, wait for your turn of course – and then the wait gets too long, too tedious, and before we know we are at the cusp of another change – caught unprepared . In the time of the perfect storm, the meaning of 'leadership' has also morphed into a new meaning – it no longer is a centralized position of power which comes with seniority of age.

One leads where he/she is an expert in – so when my seventeen year-old nephew pilots the 4-seater plane, and I trust him to land me back safely, he is my leader – for the duration of the flight. The 66 minute flight that I took with him last year in an old tin box with wings will go down my 'brave moments of life' list. While his twitchy behaviour inside the plane made me anxious, I followed his instructions carefully and did not 'dare' touch anything in this 30 year old relic.

I have experienced situational leadership several times within the organization in India. During our annual corporate social responsibility day, our professionals take the day off work to make an impact in their locality. While we nominate an overall lead for the event, a very prestigious role (that does not come with a corner office), there are thread leads for every non-governmental organization (NGO) that we support. It is an exceptional leadership opportunity for all of the nominated leads and they are called 'Sir' for the day.

During a customized leadership development session, a group of senior managers were being coached on everything from executive presence to team building skills to those traits that could set the true future leaders apart from those who had simply floated to the top based on tenure. One of the future leaders raised his hand – *"Leadership is still about getting the corner office, nothing has changed really since the time of our dads."* I couldn't deny that many of the corner offices are restricted to leaders in the organization. *"What would you do differently?"* I asked. *"To start with I would shed the insecurity of - What would I do if I developed someone else to take my job?"* Thought provoking, and this guy turned out to be quite a lateral thinker and a popular leader in his team. *"He listens end to end."*, a member of his team had once confided in me. But leadership in the new India is more than the corner office and certainly more than a heavy title.

The desire of the next generation to demonstrate their leadership skills much earlier in their careers was highlighted during a visit to one of the premier engineering schools in India. I got to interact with a bunch of kids itching to enter the work force. I was thinking through the several topics that I could speak to them about career development, life as a consultant and transitioning from campus to corporate life. In return I learnt a few lessons about leadership from 'twenty somethings'.

Sitting in the campus atriums in their track pants and *chappals*, one carried a copy of Noam Chomsky – one wouldn't quickly be able to place them in C suites in a three piece. Some were planning to jump into a lucrative industry, a few were going to their family business, a few brave hearts would start an enterprise of their own, and a few admitted that a university stint ensured a platform for their professional lives. I was waiting for at least one of them to mention that she/he wanted to become a great leader. Of course that, I was corrected, just that it is no more than a simple trophy around your neck. This group does not aspire to simply become a leader sometime late into their careers, they are aspiring to instill leadership through their future organizations and at all stages of their journey. It was not about the title and rank, it was about leading through their careers. That was an amazing idea, that leadership is not the destination but leadership skills can be situational at campus, in project teams, navigating family politics and yes, perhaps leading to a corner office with a view.

Back in the office, I often see a bunch of young professionals in animated discussions in the break outs or cafeteria. Few of them are certainly leaders in making and most are already demonstrating leadership skills within their spectrums of influence. As I watch them busy on *Whatsapp* and in parallel, with the same agility, discussing in detail about what they need to do to get their next project completed (the way they can mesh professional and personal can be a useful executive education session for middle aged leaders). I wonder what kind of leaders we are going to see by 2025 (stretching the vision a bit more than the now overused 2020 yardstick).

In another incident, I was talking to a young professional, in my mind a future leader, who was on an onsite project in the US. *"Any challenges in working out here as opposed to working back at home in India?"* I asked him sensing he was acting aloof. Twenty years ago if a partner at the firm asked me a question like that, I would have analyzed and over-thought a response. *"Where is he going with that question?"* *"What if I say that I am not facing any challenges?"* *"Would he think that I was over-*

confident?" "What could I do to give a response that would be etched in his mind?"

He simply came back with – *"Not really other than a few daily project issues. At the end of the day, I am willing to work hard as long as I am learning something and it is fun."*

My take-away from many of these conversations is that formal leadership roles are losing their lustre. It is simply taking too long to get there for this new generation. The 'hero-leader' is disappearing and respect will need to continually be earned. Current leaders in the proverbial 'corner offices' will need to adapt and provide the right environment and meaningful work and opportunities for *Gen Yers* to demonstrate 'situational' leadership. The need for general supervision with little value add will disappear.

I cannot count the number of times that I have seen this in India where you have supervisors, albeit in more labour intensive settings, standing around supervising another fellow who is actually doing the digging. Zero value add. As literacy rates increase, even the labour class in India will start pushing back.

The *Gen Yers* will continue to demand more accountability and be more transparent themselves – their world after all is mostly in the open any which way, just a click away as you can see by simply searching through their social networking sites.

The workplace was a healthy melting pot of the disciplined *Gen Xers* and the dissident millennial, the strengths of one was perhaps the weak spot of the other – they were drawing from each other, albeit a bit of reservation – *"Look at the way he speaks, sheer irreverence."* *"Man, which century solution are we talking about!"* I learnt to make peace with both sides.

This set of blogs really summarizes the various aspects of leadership – from having empathy to connecting with people. The ability to listen is a critical element of leadership. Other themes of leadership that I have witnessed are what I would term the 'intangibles' – persons who are able to carry themselves and seem to attract followers. Many leaders have a natural charisma that is able to attract the crowds. Leadership in many professions is about people management as talent plays a critical role especially in the current Indian landscape. Finally in today's landscape the topic of ethics and responsibility is becoming an emerging topic that future Indian leaders will have to focus on especially if they are to motivate and attract the *Gen Yers.*

May 2012, 6.30 p.m, Tuesday,…..School lobby, Mumbai, waiting for son's performance

1. Tell Me Your Story, All Calls on Hold – Empathy

A few months ago, during my annual health check-up (a necessary ritual when you are on the wrong side of 45), I had to fill out a rather tedious form about my medical history, exercise routine (I typically take more than a moment to reflect on this one), current medications, etc. Finally, I came upon a section – 'Addictions'?

Smoking? I proudly entered NO. Drinking? I ticked the 'Occasionally' box. Though I must admit that after coming to

India, I have developed a fondness for Scotland's favourite!

Over dinner, I proudly declared to the family how pleased I was to have almost a clean slate @ Addiction. To my surprise, they erupted in unison and pointed to the harmless looking device lying next to me …. my beloved Blackberry.

*So am I really a BB ADDICT? It is such a harsh word … **"Addiction"**. Well, if you go by the data points, I must confess I do qualify:*

- *I can text at 'bead speed' (at times when I am engrossed in texting … sure looks like am on the rosary)*
- *My hearing power has accentuated to catch even the mildest vibrating alert in maximum din.*
- *I get up 3-4 four times every night, bleary-eyed, just to see the BB glow.*

I try to convince myself that I am actually addicted to work and not the 'device'; that I simply like to be on top of things; that I like to stay in touch; that I can't afford for things to blow up in my face; that my work and home life do sometimes get blurred and its ok because I am doing a fine balancing act….. and that in this stimulating journey, my 'crackberry' is my connector, my work-companion of sorts….

But the truth is regrettably not so, and I quickly learnt that the argument falls flat … both at home and at work. As with other addictions, a BB addiction is damaging.

Recently, while conducting an interview, my BB buzzed thrice. I answered it TWO times. On noticing the disturbed look on the face of the interviewee, the whole 'Addict' allegation struck me like a 2x4 between the eyes. My addiction to my 'device' was not allowing my interviewee to "tell her story".

And that by not "listening to her story" with empathy and connect, I was losing out on a good candidate. I let the third buzz go.

Realization struck, back home too. One evening, when I got back from one of those regular trips to Hyderabad, my kids were all excited about their upcoming summer break … they wanted to "share their story". I dared to think I could multi-task … and tried the single 'thumb entry' on my BB. My boys simply walked away.

I took those learnings to a recent conversation with a client. We were all ready with our decks, to talk about our "incredible India success story" - which I can recount even in my sleep! Five minutes into "the talk", I stopped. Told myself, "Let the client tell their story". I quickly realized that projects are not won with decks and qualifications, they are won by connections, empathy, responsiveness and inquiry ……. by listening to the other side.

So, as you those times when you have to engage in those critical counselee-counsellor discussions, here is a thought for the counsellors – Before you begin the conversation, take your smartphone out of your pocket/purse and show your counselee that you are 'turning it off' … And then focus on letting your counselee 'tell their story'.

Meanwhile, I will continue to believe that BBs are one of the best inventions ever … For one thing it has quickly allowed me to write this blog while waiting in the lobby of my son's school. You see, they have a dance performance this evening… and now with this done … I can go and "see him tell his story"….

Nov 2011, back home after a couple of golf swings

2. The Green Jacket – The intangibles

Green isn't an easy colour to sport. Ask any fashionista.

Yet, one green jacket is much coveted.

The annual Masters Tournament held in Augusta, Georgia, in the U.S. is more than a prestigious event in the international golf calendar; it's sacrosanct. The winner of this tournament receives a green jacket, among other awards. The classic three-button style, single-breasted jacket with an Augusta National Golf Club logo on the left pocket, symbolizes membership to a very exclusive club – the crème de la crème of champions. Golfers train a lifetime for just that one opportunity to wear that green coat. It's a matter of envy, pride, privilege, and also ambition. I think it actually comes with a halo!

Earlier this month, I watched Angel Cabrera slip into the green jacket. It was a perfect fit. As the applause in the audience grew louder, his face reflected only one emotion – complete joy. Angel Cabrera, the school dropout-turned caddie-turned professional had arrived! History will remember him as one of the Masters' champions. It was awe-inspiring. Wearing the green jacket is not about winning or losing, it's about seeking the greatest possible glory.

Fitting into the jacket *– Around appraisal time each year, some will be seeking promotions, while others will continue with their climb. Winning the green jacket shows that while metrics are important as scoring under par is in golf, it takes more than that to 'fit' the jacket. After years* *of watching the Masters, I am amazed that every jacket fits just right!*

Like professional golf, 'fitting into the jacket' or getting to that next level and eventually reaching the pinnacle of the organization requires more than metrics. It requires an attitude in addition to natural ability.

Feb, 2012, Mumbai, before going to bed after watching some music award on T.V with sons

3.   *The Sirius Effect – Charisma*

Would you ever compare Lady Gaga and the late Mother Teresa? Blasphemous? Far-fetched?

Well, I remember reading an article in **The Economist***, a while back, which projected Lady Gaga and Mother Teresa as the latest icons of the leadership industry! Chalk and cheese in their personalities and purpose, yet, you cannot deny that both are hugely famous, sought and adored by millions, a brand in themselves.*

What works? The maverick and the messiah have one thing in common – 'Charisma'.

The 'C' factor is often thought of as an elusive ingredient, found in larger than life personalities from the worlds of politics, sports, business and entertainment. In an organization, charisma adds to the power of your personal brand and it expands your sphere of influence – none can deny this. But is charisma really synonymous with super-star status, where only the perfect swagger, the best jokes, the coolest wardrobe, the last word matter? I do not think so...

To me, charisma implies more than just style, personality, visibility and confidence. Much of it is made up of a positive chemistry, which leaves your clients, your peers, your seniors, your subordinates feeling better after interacting with you. A charismatic person is one who exudes optimism and self-confidence (which can be as subtle like Mother Teresa), so that it rubs off on those around, leaving them feeling better about themselves. Nothing can be more charismatic! (Can't help adding a quote here by Mother Teresa – "Let no one ever come to you without leaving happier.") The way we make others feel totally influences whether we have a great team, a satisfied client, a great business deal. It has been my personal experience that you never feel tired in the presence of a charismatic person with positive energy. In contrast, think of those conversations you have had, after which you felt drained out!

For a few lucky souls, charisma is a natural ingredient of their personality, it is their DNA. And while it is a blessing to be bestowed with the fairy-dust of charisma, I believe it can be learned and developed over time, and with experience. As a professional on the floor, you may need to work at your abilities to emotionally and socially connect with others. Start with, maybe, just a smile, building empathy, taking an authentic interest in others, giving sincere compliments, spreading positive energy, or at least diffusing negative energy. So, build on charisma bit by bit, brick by brick. Here, again I am tempted to use a line by Lady Gaga – "I am trying to change the world, one sequin at a time."

Often, charisma implies having a 'silver tongue', but it is also about being a great listener. A charismatic team leader takes cues from others and often helps others overcome their inhibitions. He/she has the confidence of a superstar, and at other times shows the humility of a sage; is simultaneously assertive and collaborative ... and all this without turning the risk of growing boorish or self-obsessed.

Of course, you can never undermine the importance of subject matter expertise and market-ready 'technical' skills.

Charisma or not, you need to know your score well. But it is also true that all the good ideas and the best degrees in the world won't get you far if you aren't compelling enough to convince people to listen to you and connect with you at several levels.

Finally, you may choose to be charismatic and lead full-throat (like Lady Gaga) or lead quietly (like Mother Teresa) – at the end of the day it is about leading with conviction and integrity, leading effortlessly, sometimes leading unconventionally... but always in an exemplary 'fashion'... Now fashion is an area where even I am finding it difficult to connect the dots between these two icons!

July 2011, After a great matinee show

4.   Spidey's Right

Spiderman's a superhero.

He has the ability to crawl on walls and ceilings, has superhuman strength, an acute sixth sense as well as fantastic speed and agility. He swings over New York's skyline rescuing the city and its people from evil …

*However, he wasn't always a saviour. While the bite of a genetically modified spider gave Peter Parker, a.k.a Spidey, incredible powers, it came with no instruction manual. Clueless about its application, he thought he'd exploit his powers to get rich. The death of his guardian Uncle Ben at the hands of a burglar, who Peter had not bothered to pursue, scripted the turning point in his story. The guilt of not using his powers to apprehend the burglar plagued him. He learnt a painful but life-altering lesson – **with great power comes great responsibility**. Thus Spiderman, the crime-fighter and protector was born.*

To some degree, we all have power – to influence and change the course of our lives and those around us. There are some limits, checks, and balances to that power. Most importantly, without each one of us taking personal responsibility, it can lead to undesired – and potentially fatal – outcomes.

I am reminded of this 'power' every day.

Power involves tremendous responsibility. Do not use it lightly. Remember Spiderman's credo.

Dec 2011, Parent's place, Canada

5.   *The Shackleton Odyssey – In the face of challenge*

The following is perhaps the oldest and most-often repeated leadership story. Surprisingly, it retains its relevance, significance and message to this day. Also, it never fails to motivate or energize me.

On December 5, 1914, Sir Ernest Shackleton set sail to Antarctica with a crew of 27 men aboard a ship ironically named Endurance. He was an accomplished explorer who had almost touched the South Pole, earlier in 1909. The ambition was to be the first to cross the Antarctic.

Unfortunately, in January 1915, their ship was trapped in the pack ice of the Weddell Sea. For nine months, they drifted helplessly with the ice. Then, another disaster struck. The Endurance began to sink. All the crew could save was three lifeboats, and some equipment and provisions. When food supplies dwindled, they hunted penguins and other sea life. They kept drifting in the open ocean, until they touched soil in April 1916. They had managed to reach the uninhabited Elephant Island.

Civilization was still at large. Therefore, a week later, Shackleton with five handpicked members left the island to seek help at South Georgia Island, a staggering 650 miles away. Almost 16 days later, after battling ferocious weather and treacherous water, they reached ashore. The only hitch – they were on wrong side of the island, the uninhabited side.

Bereft of any choice, Shackleton with two men decided to reach their destination on foot. This meant crossing the mountainous, glaciated, and the uncharted interior of the island. Finally, on May 20, 1916, they walked into the whaling station at Stromness Bay. It would be another four months and three attempts before Shackleton could rescue his stranded team members from the Elephant Island. Amazingly, in these two years, not one life was lost.

The team beat all odds to survive to tell the tale. It is widely credited to be Shackleton's triumph as a leader. Here are some of my thoughts (in no particular order) for you to ponder:

- *Leaders always seek newer and challenging assignments. Shackleton set a new Antarctic challenge. He actually popularized polar exploration.*
- *Ambition is a perquisite for leaders. However, it also needs vision, mission and commitment. Shackleton had definite goals, mission and was committed throughout the journey.*
- *Leaders are always experts in their subject matter. This calls for a lot of hard work and dedication to get 'above the bar'. Shackleton was experienced in polar exploration. His knowledge and skills helped the team throughout the two years.*
- *Leaders constantly communicate with their teams. Shackleton shared every small change in the plan with this team. They were always a part of the plan.*
- *Leaders have to be flexible. Even watertight plans need a backup. Shackleton remained flexible in his tactics throughout the journey. Depending on the vagaries of the environment, he kept tweak-*

ing his plan. At one point, his sole ambition was to keep every member on the expedition alive.

- *Leaders care about people. They put people first. Despite his burning ambition, Shackleton abandoned his quest. His sense of responsibility towards his team was stronger. Success lies not only in reaching your chosen destination – but also living to tell the tale.*

- *Leaders are optimistic. Despite the miserable cold, wetness, fatigue and hunger, he remained optimistic and so was every member on his team.*

- *Leaders always develop the next generation of leaders. Shackleton created strong leaders within his team. Hence, the team survived even when he wasn't physically around to lead them.*

- *Leaders lead by example. Shackleton also took turns to perform the most menial of chores. He made things happen. Actions speak louder than words.*

- *Leaders take failures in their stride. Shackleton and his men never even set foot on Antarctic. Instead of being labeled a failure, Shackleton is a celebrated as a true leader.*

Being a leader is neither complex nor impossible. There is a Shackleton in each one of us. We need to unleash him.

*October 2012, Hotel in Pennsylvania.. after a week
of strategic leadership training*

6. *Walking the Fields of Gettysburg – brevity and powerful conversations*

The past week and half has been much about family time (I like to believe …a well-deserved break), work sandwiched in between as usual, a brush with history, and some timeless lessons in brevity.

I attended a leadership training at the Army War College in Pennsylvania. The programme touches upon various facets of leadership - ethics, communication, vision, intricacies and challenges of decision-making etc.

One topic stayed with me in particular – the power of words.

During those two days at the college, we re-traced the events of the American Civil War at Gettysburg - a place where the **"future of America's freedom hung in balance."** The killing fields of Gettysburg are further immortalized by Abraham Lincoln's famous The Gettysburg Address often called the only speech delivered that day. That's a misnomer because Edward Everett, a nationally famous orator, was assigned the main address while Lincoln delivered the Dedicatory remarks. Everett's speech, which took **two** hours, witnessed a restless crowd, as the attendees started to wander about the fields made memorable by the fierce struggles of July 1863.

In contrast, Lincoln's address lasted for a **few minutes.** It was observed that, "the great assembly listened, almost *awe-struck, as to a voice from the divine oracle." Despite popular stories, historians agree that Lincoln did not whip up his 'remarks' on the back of an envelope en route from Washington. It was the product of a lifetime, from a man known for his study and deep reflection.*

I also learnt that the Generals on the battlefield had to make prompt decisions, often without complete information, and communicate it to other stations over the din of mayhem (communications 'technologies' were surely at a premium). So, they had to choose their words very carefully … as did Lincoln.

Now consider this – The U.S. Constitution is only 12 pages long… the EU Constitution is 300 …. Obama's Healthcare reform package is 1900! This thought came as a flash, as I stood in front of the White House – part of the holiday promise made to my kids, my younger one a self-proclaimed Obama fan.

The world has become a lot more complicated, but seriously!

Closer to home and present: Think about the volume and velocity of modern communications – but honestly how much of those conversations do we really take home? Our email boxes overflow, yet we are still searching for an answer at the end of every day. We carry our mobiles to the grocery stores so that we can call our spouses to confirm the type of bread to buy … staring at the wall of new found options.

We need to let go of words…..

I believe that in our work too, we can strive to 'talk' less and 'say' more. Running an effective model in the on-site / off-shore space requires us to abridge the 30 minutes conversations down to 15, and the 15 to 5.

Try this:

- *Cut the fluff—Come to the point.*
- *Use active voice—Be owners of your conversations*
- *Use more inductive (your experiences) versus deductive (general principles) reasoning*
- *Jump to the punch line and then go on and defend your point of view as required*
- *Spare the other side the burden of jargons—clean up the 'buzz' before hitting send*
- *Brevity YES—but not at the altar of clarity*

That day at Gettysburg, I realized, that among other things, Leadership requires an ongoing conversation – a simple one with a deep meaning.

Meanwhile, I am experimenting with the quintessential 140 characters of making conversations ….

January 2011, Delhi Airport waiting lounge

7.   Home Truths about People Management

The famed winter chill is absent, as I head out of the Delhi airport. While I have been to the nation's capital plenty of times before, this trip was special. I was accompanying the dean of my MBA school on her first trip to India. She was here to examine and understand the deeper realities of India's talent dynamics. I must confess, the assignment made me feel proud, privileged, and a tad nervous, too.

As we hit the road, the day was a blur with meetings with educational institutes and global corporations. Just before lunch, a parting comment by a senior executive took me by surprise. "You are in the business of people. You must like being surrounded by people all the time, very much," he remarked. Nodding in the affirmative, I had moved on to the next meeting on our agenda. However, his words lingered in the back of my mind.

People relationships are indeed at the core of everything we do every day. This reality hit home hard again, a few hours later. We met the country head of a major bank to discuss his expectations from a talent perspective. Instead of needing a lot more smart people to come up with new derivative products, he was looking for people who could negotiate, collaborate, lead, and inspire. In short, he wanted people who could team with other people to achieve desired results.

While mulling over their observations on my flight back, I recalled an anecdote that I read a long time ago. It had made quite an impression on me. American billionaire Andrew

Carnegie hired Charles Schwab as the President of U.S. Steel for $1 million. Well, this was in 1921! Surprisingly, the big salary was not for his technical expertise, but his ability to motivate. Charles' greatest asset was his ability to arouse enthusiasm among his people. This remarkable gift helped him lead labour union-free corporations in his lifetime.

Nearly nine decades later, our people skills still define us. Yet, society largely ignores its importance in our lives. No university even has a course on this topic! We perceive these 'soft skills' are either inborn or too complicated to master. True, it comes easier to a few. However, effective people management skills can be learnt, irrespective of your personality.

*It is a fact that we share our success or failures more effortlessly than knowledge. Our insecurities inhibit us from making collaborations a way of life. I strongly believe that Consulting is a team sport. **There are no individual superstars**. Sure, we need to have accountability and continue to drive numbers – sales, revenues, profits …. But, without your ability to connect and collaborate with each other (using soft skills), it will be impossible to deliver the hard numbers.*

This means having implicit faith in the abilities of other people. Of course, they will fail from time to time. Nevertheless, you have to continue believing and encouraging them. Their success should be equally important as yours. I think, the art of praise is not lost, albeit neglected. A simple (and sincere) 'thank you', 'great job', or 'well done' can go a long way. It is a powerful motivator, making people feel valued and inclusive. Money isn't always the greatest motivator. **Remember, people do not leave organizations. People just leave people.**

Also, listen instead of just hearing. Multi-tasking is making listening a dying art. Next time, try this approach: Shut down your mailbox, silence the cell phone, and focus on the person opposite you. Make them feel good about themselves. Most importantly, treat people the way you want to be treated. That's the essence of people management.

Finally, for the record, in case you were wondering, I really do enjoy being around people.

4.2   Final Reflections – What next? Who next?

Mackerel skies and mares tails, soon will be time to shorten sails

In September 2013, I was transitioning out of a formal leadership position that I had held for eight years, and I was getting ready for a new role. Our matrix organization ensures that leadership titles are only about a next set of responsibilities versus ladder scrambling. So, as I stood on the threshold of my 'next', my anxiety was mostly around how prepared I was really to dive into my next role (a challenging one which still lacked structure or resemblance to anything I was used to – seemed more like a start-up to me really). In India especially, like other emerging markets, organizations will continue to break new ground and define new tracks. In the case of my role, I was going to define the tracks along the way. Sure to be a lot of fun, but I felt that I had been down this road before.

My first day reminded me of that day at Mumbai airport when I landed in India (or for that matter when the family and I landed in Beijing and frankly even when my wife and I touched down at Kai Tak airport in Hong Kong back in August of 1995). One is never quite prepared ever, it's just that the 'new waters' keep getting deeper and choppier perhaps.

During a conversation with my wife who perceived a sense of restlessness and asked me point blank, *"Do you know what you will be doing?"* I retorted, *"I guess so …"*.

It was simply to figure out how to serve our most important global clients in India. How difficult could that be?

Ask any leader, how much ever seasoned, handing over the baton to the next is always challenging. More so at a time when the world at large is grappling to find the next generation of leaders – talk to anyone in business, politics or someone who bears the cross of creating the next cadre of leaders for the society. In India the crisis deepens against the Perfect Storm scenario. Companies perhaps could not keep pace with a decade of exponential growth, when it came to growing their leadership pipelines.

I met a global leader of a major bank who had several thousands of professionals working for her in India. She said that while they had accomplished what they wanted to by investing in India, it was time for them to move to the next stage. The challenge for her in her own words was – *"Who next? Where is my next bunch of leaders?"* Her leadership on the ground was coasting and she did not see the potential for them to take their India investment to the next level. Getting there required Indian leaders on the ground to view India in a different light and see their role as broader than being a 'caretaker' on the ground.

I experienced this first hand when trying to source such leaders from the market for our organization. Most dwelled about their past and glorious histories, accomplishments and titles as opposed to talking about what they could do for us in the future. They would recount how many people were reporting to them in their earlier roles. *"So what can you do for me?"*, I would usually ask them. *"How have you inspired the new Gen Yers at your workplace?"* My sense is that many of them have simply been pushed along by the 'demographic dividend wave', while several were unfortunately going to be swallowed up by the tide.

For this cadre of leaders (presumably in their mid-40s to early 50s), when they started their careers, the storm was only faintly visible on the horizon. Back then, there was no ambiguity, guidelines were planned out and there was a beaten path to follow. Everyone had a role to play, that was clearly defined and while perhaps technically challenging, over time the roles were understood and the skills to perform the roles were learned. Ambitions were in place but one didn't have the markers to visualize the storm, let alone emerge from it on the other side.

Suddenly workplaces (more so in the IT/ITeS sector) looked up to those who could manage technology versus manage people around them. The conventional leaders, who were till then nestling in their comfort zones, leading by the book, were suddenly jostled. I have come across various kinds of managers, leaders-in-waiting – the forerunners one day. All kinds they were – those that effortlessly connected with people over cricket talk, those who continuously prepared themselves, those that were unable to come to terms with 'takeovers', those that were in denial... One thing struck me even that early – here was a lot that were sandwiched between the more austere early *Gen Xers* and Baby Boomers who had led them, and the more aggressive millennial. Some of them, during the storm, got pushed into leadership roles for which they were perhaps not fully prepared. But there were no questions asked given their tenure.

In the perfect storm, the new generation has no reservations about questioning your decisions, challenging the *status quo* and escalating when they witness any lapses in accountability. And when the corner offices turn into a fish bowl ....you either swim or sink.

The most fulfilling part of my journey in India has been seeing business leaders emerge through this storm over the past several years. They have been a bit bruised and battered, but they have endured, taken risks, continued to learn, changed tactics and have worked the 'new' rules of navigating the storm.

Thinking back on my journey, I frankly could not have envisaged this outcome in which several global leaders were emerging from our organization back in 2005.

Back then in the middle of the storm, India was 'dot com on steroids'. It was about taking advantage of labour arbitrage, about leveraging junior talent that cost a fraction of what new graduates would. The notion about creating leaders based in India, not to mention those with a global mindset and ones willing to take risks and captain ships in global storms was not even on the radar.

There was no demand issue to keep people busy in India-based delivery centres. 'Leaders' were taking orders. The 'caretakers' were simply responding to phones.... 'How many people do you need?' 'By the way, do you want fries with that?' Life was good. Looking back, though hectic, it was the momentary calm before the storm.

A few years into the role, it hit me like a boom swinging around a ship, *"Why can we not make global leaders sitting in India? In fact, we'll be dead if we do not!"* But we had not thought in depth what this 'India leader' looked like.

In our partnership model, it is all about making the right impressions in front of our clients. Leaders in our business were directly engaged with clients either selling and/or delivering great work. Relationships were built over time. Typically though, the lead person sitting in India was 'anonymous' to the client. The reality was that we would get the call to provide support much after the client relationship had been developed. There was little chance for those on the ground in India to demonstrate personality here or develop deep client engagement, critical to making leaders in our organization.

There was though something brewing on the horizon as this storm was taking another twist. From our lens, we could sense the tide shifting. As more and more work was being delivered on India's shores, the need for true leadership was growing, not just 'caretaker' leadership, who are simply guiding traffic, but real leadership making critical decisions and taking risks. The expectations from Indian leaders had begun to churn and evolve.

It was not until we witnessed a major milestone in our journey that the need for leadership in India truly came to light. A major client said that they would be visiting India before deciding to award a new contract to us and they wanted to see the people who were doing the real work on the ground ... ones with Indian business cards. They wanted an India-based leader, whose 'throat they could choke'.

And then the India based leader definition began to emerge.

.... And for those emerging leaders, it is now on their shoulders to define the path for the others to follow. If they make the choice to let those behind them struggle as some of them might have, many will be lost in the storm. India is not in a position to accept this fate. It is not an option. They have to leave an easier trail for the next generation. While India has exported many leaders around the world, those who won the 'visa lottery' ticket, the country now needs leadership at home.

As for me, I look behind at at confident teams and able leaders that have grown around me, and I look ahead at my unfinished task at hand – to spot, raise and celebrate so many more of tomorrow's leaders.

Gaudi's Canvas – The job is never done

If you have ever been to Barcelona, you can't have missed the exuberant, the eccentric, and the sky-line defining *Sagrada Familia*—a Roman Catholic church, considered as a masterpiece of the famous Spanish architect Antoni Gaudì. The construction of this heritage basilica started in 1882, and the official completion date is said to be around 2028! An ongoing project of 140 years. A piece of history in continuum!

A couple of years ago, on a holiday to Barcelona with family, I visited this most curious and celebrated work of art. Tourists thronged the place, while the strewn plaster molds and mortar signaled work in progress. The cranes and scaffolding on the spires and the polychrome glass windows, made me realize why Gaudi had once remarked: "My client (read God) is not in a hurry….". He worked for 40 years on this one project…before handing it over to the next generation to continue on it, enhance it … his 'life's work'.

A promotion/next level is certainly an exciting milestone in one's career, quite a trophy moment, sort of defines the pinnacle of the profession. Though, as with Gaudi's 'canvas', it is work in progress. A newly appointed leader's 'life's work' has actually just begun *again*, though perhaps from a new perspective or elevation - always a new spire here, a brand new foyer to add there, more bannisters for the façade, more intricate woodwork on the ceiling.....working on an ever-changing blueprint of never-ending details. That's how you leave behind a *Sagrada Familia* for the future generation.

The *Sagrada* actually throws up some interesting leadership co-relations -

- Like Gaudi, a true leader conceives a project or a vision, gives it his/her 100 percent, fully knowing that the legacy has to be handed over to another generation.

- A leader always works amidst a lot of uncertainty, and manages changing environment, stakeholders and client priorities – The *Sagrada Familia* was always in a state of 'beta' project. And, the challenges spanned the Spanish Civil War to recent hazards of constructing a high-speed train tunnel nearby.

- The leader focusses on details, never losing sight of the big picture – Like Gaudi, constantly working on two palettes – the micro details and the macro vision.

- The leader is humble – Gaudi never let his structure be taller than a local peak considered holy. He said no man-made creation should surpass God's creation.

- A leader should sometimes be audacious and go after the stretch goals – Like Gaudi, beat the normal, add the baroque to the somber, throw in some gravity-defying ideas.

As I think about the accomplishments of pioneering women, I reflect on the fate of *Sagrada*, had Gaudi been a woman. I can safely wager that given the innate ability of women to juggle, prioritize and simply get things done, the Sagrada would have been completed by now! (and Gaudi would have also raised *her* own children in parallel)

Afterword

Now bring me that horizon

From harbour to horizon – it has been a wild sail through the Perfect Storm. The past few years have given me a once in a lifetime opportunity to witness India's fairy tale growth, more specifically the rise and spread of Gen Next who are clearly redefining the workplace.

While I have come through and am moving into a new storm, I was one of the lucky ones who entered the storm in a captain's uniform with guides and tools to get me through, I will relish this experience. Parts of the journey were stormy for me, and in parts the north winds sailed me home. I held fast to my compass, I knew how to get help when required, I had some inkling of what was waiting on the other side of the storm (old weathered captain!) – yet the satisfaction of having not only emerged from the storm myself, but also to have guided several others along the journey is something else. So is leaving behind many more hands to take charge at the helm.

The next few years are going to be even more exciting for India as a groundswell of passion and pride continues to drive significant political change and upheaval. But to truly drive India to its well-deserved position in the world hierarchy, this demographic dividend will have to take charge and lead from the front. And not to add more pressure, but this lot can't afford to fail given their sheer size. The implications will in fact be quite dramatic. And they won't fail, I say. I have seen the responsibility they exude even if they are not looking at me and busy rolling their fingers over smart phones. One thing is for sure – they won't hang unsuccessful and India needs that kind of energy right now.

For this generation, all I can say is that the rewards that are waiting for you are tremendous and greater than even I can see. It will continue to be a complicated, in places a treacherous journey but I hope that this book helps you make some of the right navigation decisions and puts into perspective those decisions that might not go as anticipated. For the generation ahead, perhaps there is a bit in it for you as well.

For me, well I am just starting another journey, to get beyond 'India for beginners' as I have jokingly referred to my past few years (well, perhaps, that was an exaggeration). The next storm is new but if I am able to learn from my own advice and look to the newly emerging leaders, the sail should be pretty smooth.

Acknowledgements

Finally, a few acknowledgements (as a first time author I am both thrilled and nervous about this part).

I want to thank those several colleagues and friends at work who knowingly or unknowingly gave me ideas for my blogs over coffee or in a meeting room. While there are too many to name, a few of them know who they are and hopefully will remember the interactions that led to an idea for a blog.

Shobha Ramaswamy, a former colleague, who got me started and bombed my 'writer's block'. Monidipa Mukherjee who saw the possibility of this book even before me and acted as a referee throughout.

Gautam Padmanabhan and Karthik Venkatesh from Westland for talking a leap of faith with a debutant.

Finally, my two boys Pranav and Arjun and wife Vandana for being part of this journey and simply enjoying the scenery along the road.